A Field Guide to
Trains
of North America

A Field Guide to

Trains

of North America

Gerald L. Foster

HOUGHTON MIFFLIN COMPANY

Boston   New York

1996

For information about this and other Houghton Mifflin
trade and reference books and multimedia products, visit
The Bookstore at Houghton Mifflin on the World Wide Web at
http://www.hmco.com/trade/.

Library of Congress Cataloging-in-Publication Data
Foster, Gerald L.
A field guide to trains of North America/Gerald L. Foster.
p.   cm.
Includes index.
ISBN 0-395-70112-0
1. Railroads — United States.   I. Title.
TF23.F68   1996
625.2' 0973--dc20   95-44168

Printed in the United States of America

HAD 10 9 8 7 6 5 4 3 2 1

Contents

Introduction   vii

Identifying Diesel and Electric Locomotives   1

End-Cab Switchers   6

Road Switchers/Low Hood   20

Road Switchers/High Hood/B-B (four-axle)   26

Road Switchers/High Hood/C-C (six-axle)   50

Road Switcher/Wide Nose/B-B (four-axle)   74

Road Switcher/Wide Nose/C-C (six-axle)   78

Full-Width Hood   88

Full-Width Hood/"Draper Taper"   106

Electrics   110

Trainsets   116

Passenger Cars   118

Freight Cars   122

Glossary   131

Life List   133

Acknowledgments and Further Reading   135

Index   137

Introduction

Railroads in general and locomotives in particular continue to fascinate many of us, as they have for generations, despite major upheavals in the rail industry over time. Steam power and the culture of massive mechanical machinery, for example, gave way in the 1940s to diesel engines and electric drive systems. More recently, mergers have combined major railroads of the past into huge conglomerates that abandon or sell off unprofitable (to them) branch lines. Some of those branch lines have occasionally become small railroads themselves, serving and maintaining local connections and markets. Today U.S. passenger trains edge toward extinction, yet freight hauling sets new records yearly while national rail mileage continues to decline. These developments continually call for new equipment and strategies to serve the railroad scene.

As railroading evolves new forms, sounds, and smells, our fascination continues as well, perhaps because railroads are that part of American heavy industry that is visible to us outside the walls and chainlink fences of factories, industrial parks, and power plants. Unless we are personally involved in heavy industry, the locomotive, because of its mobility, is probably the largest piece of industrial equipment most of us will see. It enables two or three people — in hands-on style — to move great amounts of our society's material wealth long distances — from raw materials to finished goods. And it has an impressive visual impact: massive, powerful, and expressive of its purpose, whether that may be pulling a 100-car coal train out of West Virginia or sorting boxcars at the freight yards in Moberly, Missouri.

In the late steam era, locomotives displayed their wonderful mechanical ingenuity on the outside for all to see — the massive boiler and smokebox, the cylinders, the beautiful valve gear, rods, and drivers — all amid smoke and steam and noise, and, in the case of large engines, the minuscule cab at the rear with its levers and gauges just ahead of the tender, the rolling fuel and water supply. The uniquely powerful character of late American steam engines grew out of innovative configurations of the 19th century, which were developed to deal with difficult American conditions: long distances, steep grades, sharp curves, and poor track. These distinctive locomotives evolved into the impressive monsters of the 20th century, still uniquely American when compared to contemporary European designs, towing ever larger loads but also growing in mechanical complexity and amount of stress on the machinery and on the track itself. Few aesthetic considerations intruded into the engineering of these marvelous creations. Their beauty and elegance was determined by function, utility, and the properties of the metals they were made of.

But in a brief 20-year period from about 1940 to 1960, this century-old concept of steam locomotive design, rooted in blacksmith shop and steel mill technology, was displaced by a new concept that combined internal combustion and electricity. This astonishing revolution (which some say would have happened even faster had not World War II intervened) changed the look of railroading, or at least the locomotive end of the train, and a great many railfans have yet to recover. The diesel-electric locomotive required only a platform large enough for the prime mover (the diesel engine), some electrical equipment, and a cab for the crew (which still included a fireman). Small fuel tanks hung below the platform and replaced the separate fuel tender. All this rode on simple trucks of smallish wheels the size of the pilot or trailing truck wheels on steam locomotives. Several of these wheels were driven by small traction motors, all but invisible in the truck assembly. Visually, as well as technically, this was a complete departure from what had gone before and was certainly less appealing to the eye and the ear of many observers. Although the streamlined diesels did provide ideal surfaces for colorful and distinctive paint schemes, introducing a new aesthetic to the American landscape, they were a jolt to the traditional railroader. More significantly however, the diesels required far less maintenance and were easier on the rails. This successful configuration remains the basic concept of locomotive design today.

Several manufacturers responded to the demand for this efficient new idea. Traditional builders of steam engines such as Lima, Baldwin, and the American Locomotive Company (Alco) attempted the transition to diesel power, but newer companies from other fields were attracted as well: the Electro-Motive Corporation, Fairbanks-Morse, and General Electric are familiar examples. Each of these builders adopted the typical diesel-electric concept but solved the engineering design problems in ways that became signatures of their particular shops. These are the identifying field marks I have used throughout this book to identify and classify the locomotives in use today in North America.

Not many of the builders have survived, and locomotive manufacturing in some ways has become a small business, with two manufacturers dealing with only six or eight customers. Few railroads can afford to order dozens of one- or two-million-dollar locomotives, and General Electric and General Motors compete fiercely for the business. The smaller roads are left with capable hand-me-downs and rebuilds. Thanks to the diesel engine's renowned longevity, Alcos, Baldwins, and others are still out there working, although in diminishing numbers.

The first purpose of this book is to allow anyone interested in railroading to identify and name any locomotive observed in North America that is operated by scheduled railroads, from shortlines to Class 1 organizations. Whatever is running out there *now* and earning a living hauling freight or passengers is included. Not covered are tourist railroads, museum pieces, and industrial locomotives. Each of those subjects could easily fill a separate book and probably has.

This guide is organized visually rather than historically or by manufacturer. Similar types are grouped together to aid in comparison, and the diagnostic field marks are noted for the particular model. The process is similar to that of birdwatching or airplane spotting with the use of field guides. Some field marks are obvious, making identification simple, as in the case of a Canada goose or a P-38. Other differences are as subtle as those between fall warblers or modern airliners. This book finds the subtleties and points them out — from the early F series diesels to the latest "Big Macs."

Secondly, this book calls the reader's attention to the other obvious aspect of trains — the great variety of rolling stock — and points out the types of freight and passenger cars one is likely to see. The great variation in freight cars prohibits the drawing of every car in use, but the illustrations make it possible to identify the type and use of the freight cars observed. While locomotives receive most of the attention of train watchers, much can be learned about trains by identifying the cars they pull, thus adding greater understanding and appreciation of railroad activity.

Freight car design has kept pace with the shipping industry's innovations by providing bigger and stronger cars that are also more sophisticated in their sensitivity to cargo. Precise temperature control and gentler ride are examples of this progress. New types of cars have appeared in response to new concepts such as intermodal *piggy-backing,* and long unit trains of truck trailers and shipping containers are now a common sight. Ease of maintenance and loading-unloading techniques have changed the appearance of boxcars and tankers. New requirements have added new car types such as the steel-coil car and the 89-foot-long closed auto carrier while, sadly, cabooses have all but disappeared, casualties of economic considerations and communications technology.

Passenger cars have dwindled both in number and type with the severe scaling back of passenger train service in the '60s and '70s. The interstate highway system and the network of airports built after World War II greatly increased travel in the U.S. but often at the railroads' expense. Still, passenger trains roll across the country, under Amtrak's direction in the U.S., and the eclectic collection of equipment from railroads that had abandoned unprofitable passenger service made for some interesting Amtrak consists. Some cars dating from the 1940s are still in use. Gradually, however, rebuilt cars and newer designs gave the trains the more unified appearance we now see. Despite continual financial difficulty, Amtrak is adding new equipment, particularly in the Northeast Corridor where ridership is heavy and thus profitable.

In both areas, locomotives and rolling stock, the variety is considerable and involves equipment built over half a century. The identification of this equipment thus has a certain historical context and provides a live view of the evolution of equipment design that constantly moves toward greater efficiency in a usually unselfconscious manner.

Train watching is an activity that is enjoyed by many thousands of people and that supports several sizeable enterprises involving photography, research and book publishing, model railroading, and the collecting of railroad memorabilia. It is my hope that this book will contribute to the experience and enjoyment of this rewarding pastime. It is also hoped that this book can contribute to a growing interest and appreciation of railroading and that this interest may positively affect current and future legislative decisions that will determine the fate of this valued but often neglected American institution.

A Field Guide to
Trains
of North America

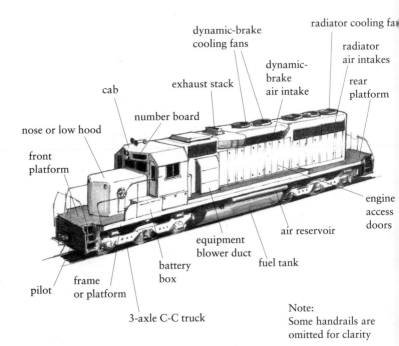

radiator cooling fan

dynamic-brake
cooling fans

radiator
air intakes

dynamic-
brake
air intake

rear
platform

exhaust stack

cab

number board

nose or low hood

front
platform

engine
access
doors

air reservoir

equipment
blower duct

fuel tank

battery
box

frame
or platform

pilot

3-axle C-C truck

Note:
Some handrails are
omitted for clarity

THE PARTS OF A LOCOMOTIVE

Identifying Diesel and Electric Locomotives

Diesel nomenclature can be confusing even to veteran train watchers and intimidating or frustrating to newcomers trying to distinguish locomotive types they run across in freight yards or model shops. Reflecting their engineering backgrounds rather than slick marketing strategies, locomotive builders have consistently relied on sequences of numbers and initials rather than names when christening their products. There are no Thunderbird or Grand Prix locomotives, nor are they named for their inventors like a Ford or a Beechcraft. There are instead F59PHIs, C44-9Ws, and SD40T-2s. (There are nicknames such as "Geeps" and "U-boats," usually coined by equipment users who presumably get tired of reciting the numbers and letters and need simpler terms for everyday use.) Identification by model number can become maddening when a manufacturer arbitrarily switches numbering systems or when a railroad attaches its own number series. Fortunately, there are those who keep track of all this for the rest of us, and I am eternally grateful to them. One of the purposes of this book is to try to give visual meaning to the designations and at least provide a place to quickly look them up.

Drawings have been used instead of photographs not only because trains are interesting and fun to draw, but because drawings allow the artist to emphasize crucial details while selecting angles and views that best indicate identifying characteristics. Extraneous detail and shadows can be eliminated to help see the form. If a handrail interferes visually with a set of louvers it can be left out. A drawing can ignore paint jobs that confuse the basic lines or obscure details (or go out of style). And proprietary details of individual railroads, such as special lighting equipment or odd horn locations, can be replaced with details more likely to be seen.

Several obvious visual aspects of diesel locomotives aid in breaking down the large number of different models into logical groups. To some extent this is historical (size, for example) and in some ways a manufacturer's designs tend to be similar, but this is not always the case. So instead of a chronological listing

1

or a chapter on each locomotive builder, I have found six configurations that include the engines in operation on scheduled railroads today. They are

> end-cab switchers
> low-hooded road switchers
> high-hooded road switchers
> wide-nosed road switchers
> full-width hood
> electrics

End cab switchers were the first diesel locomotives and followed the basic layout of the steam engines they succeeded — cab at the rear and power plant out front — logical, traditional but also a major safety consideration.

Road switchers were originally yard switchers also equipped to pull trains over the road. This usually meant more power and extra equipment such as steam generators to keep passengers warm in the older steam-heated passenger cars. Eventually a short hood was added behind the cab on end-cab switchers to house the equipment.

The first road switchers kept their hoods low and made a distinctive silhouette with their high cab roof and good crew visibility. See the Alco RS3 entry on page 20. But as more horsepower was needed hoods grew higher, as high as the cab roof eventually, but cabs couldn't grow because of clearance requirements. Visibility suffered until the short high hood became a low nose facing forward, giving us the configuration we commonly see today.

But road switchers were considered less than graceful by many, particularly when at the head of a passenger train. So while their form was evolving, more streamlined shapes that visually lined up with the passenger cars were developed. EMD's F series is a prime example. These full-width models have been called many things — car-bodies, cab units, or simply passenger locomotives. For our purposes, with the accent on visual properties, I will use the term full-width hood.

With the diminishing passenger service in the U.S., most passenger locomotives were converted for freight use or scrapped. With a few exceptions such as the "Draper Taper" design described herein, the practical, easily accessed road switcher universally displaced the streamliners. However, new interest in cleaner designs is indicated by the introduction of GE's Genesis and EMD's F59PHI.

Unlike much of the rest of the railroad world, electrified trains are rare in North America. These are trains that pick up electric power for their traction motors from an overhead wire (a catenary) or an electrified third rail. But because trains enter New York City through tunnels, and because New York has long had restrictions on train smoke and exhaust, electric locomotives are required there and are thus well known on the

Northeast Corridor from Washington to New Haven. Further expansion is anticipated to Boston. An 80-mile long branch of British Columbia Rail is also electrified north of Prince George, and some highly visible industrial mining lines in the Southwest operate electric locomotives. Accordingly, they are included here although those living outside these areas won't find them.

Any locomotive should immediately fall into one of the above visual categories, which are also indicated at the top of each illustrated page. Further, virtually all locomotives in this book ride on pairs of either four- or six-wheel trucks, referred to in the industry as B-B or C-C trucks respectively. I refer to them also as four-axle and six-axle locomotives. This is usually an instant identifying mark. My method may not entirely agree with other systems of identification, but I believe it will be found useful and consistent.

What to Look For

Most of the locomotives you find will be cab-forward, low-nosed road switchers. Then note the trucks. Are they B-B (four wheel) or C-C (six wheel)?

At this point, many locomotives may well look pretty much alike. But there are distinguishing marks as manufacturers have their typical ways of doing things. EMD prefers the graceful rounded fuel tanks but very angular cabs. GE prefers winglike top-mounted radiators at the rear of the hood while EMD's radiators are inside and cooled with a row of two, three, or four visible round exhaust fans atop the hood. These manufacturers' signatures will quickly narrow down the possibilities. More subtle are the platform frame profiles and air intakes.

Obviously, the older a locomotive, the greater the possibility that it has been modified or rebuilt, which may mean obscured or replaced original design details. Louvers, grilles, and screens can be especially deceiving. Frame profiles, on the other hand, are rarely modified and are a sure indication when other factors are uncertain. Other design characteristics such as rounded, sloped, or squared-off ends and corners usually survive customizing.

Trucks of several types are common but not reliable as field marks unless designed for a specific locomotive, such as in the case of electric locomotives. Although locomotives were shown in the catalog as equipped with a specific truck, different types of trucks from trade-ins were often used on new diesels, particularly 20 to 30 years ago when some of the most common locomotives were built.

Finally we get to items such as the number of louvers on a battery box or counting the access doors on the side of the long hoods of two otherwise identical locomotives. This may seem obsessive to some readers, but I have learned it is crucial to others. Modelers in particular are quick to note the slightest design change, whereas railroads and manufacturers often don't bother to record minor evolutionary upgrades. Hobbyists thus add their own designations as *phases* of a production run. The EMD BL2, for example, is noted for having at least two phases based on louver, handrail, and pilot details. An official at EMD is amazed and somewhat amused at the excitement caused among "rivet counters," as he calls them, by the relocation of grilles or ditch lights.

Where possible in the drawings, I have called out minor items when necessary for identification. I have de-emphasized or omitted variable items and those specific to a particular railroad, such as headlight, horn, and number-board placement, as well as pilot and snowplow detail. These can be misleading and irrelevant.

In each entry, the item or items that will absolutely identify it are pointed out whether they be as obvious as a full-width cab or as obscure as a water-level sight gauge. Beyond that I would refer researchers to the great quantity of published works that deal at length with specific locomotives and railroads.

There is another way, besides using a field guide, to identify locomotives. Up-to-date rosters list locomotives by their railroad's numbering system, and if the observer can make out the the number, usually stenciled on the cab or hood sides, he or she can then look it up and positively determine the type. James W. Kerr and Charles W. McDonald have published comprehensive rosters and I highly recommend them. The key to roster identification is the phrase *up-to-date*. Many locomotives change hands each year, particularly the older ones. As old units are retired, their numbers may be reused on new equipment. Railroads have also been known to arbitrarily change their numbering systems.

Locomotive rosters by their nature are lists of numbers and perhaps lack the satisfying visual connection of a photograph or a drawing. Nevertheless, they can be valuable identification aids, particularly for newer equipment, and I used them often in preparing this book. It is clear to me that rosters and field guides complement each other.

Pitfalls

Having claimed perfection in the preceding paragraphs, I must point out some obvious challenges. There are many, many locomotives in operation, and most of them are old with thousands of hours and millions of miles on them. They have often been passed from road to road being repaired, modified, and rebuilt along the way, some hardly resembling their original selves, and thus very difficult to identify. Total rebuilds are more common now, and there are companies such as Morrison Knudsen (MK Rail) that specialize in remanufacturing — obtaining the appropriate locomotives and rebuilding them to order. Illinois Central Railroad has rebuilt many GP7s and GP9s, renaming them with IC's own designations — GP8s, GP10s, and GP11s.

Some engines, really just a few, are hard to fit into categories,

4

but I hope they will be discovered anyway. The BL2 resembles a hooded road switcher from the rear and a full-bodied F series locomotive from the front. It uses the platform and hood construction of the high-hooded road switcher but has a partial envelope body of trusses and sheet metal. The "Draper Taper" SD40-2F is just an SD40-2 with a wider hood and a Canadian style Comfort Cab, but it looks like a full envelope body. A choice had to be made and I hope it is not confusing. This was only rarely a problem.

In the interest of simplicity, I have used "EMD" (for Electro-Motive Division), to represent the products of parent company General Motors. Distinctions are sometimes made between locomotives built in GM's facility in Ontario and their U.S. plant at La Grange, Illinois, but this is not essential for spotting purposes. Unlike the case of GE (General Electric), the parent company's initials, "GM," are not usually used in locomotive designation, whereas EMD is generally understood by all.

Some locomotives no doubt will just be missed. Perhaps there is an obscure tourist railroad out there still operating FTs or even E7s. I have no doubt I will be hearing about them, as railfans are nothing if not eager to demonstrate their watchful scrutiny of the railroad scene. I look forward to hearing from them and learning.

Alco S-1, S-2 (S-3, S-4)

Length: 45 ft. 6 in. *Horsepower:* S-1 600; S-2 1,000 *Cyl.:* 6
Date of mfr.: S-1, S-2 1940–1950; S-3 1950–1957; S-4
1950–1961 *Approx. no. built:* S-1 540; S-2 1,500; S-3 292;
S-4 782

Rounded nose with inset headlight. Square exhaust fan assembly
on top of hood over side radiator shutters. (Early and now
probably nonexistent S-1s and S-2s had a round exhaust fan recessed in the top of the hood.) Handrail is sideframe mounted
with eight stanchions. Cab has curved windows over the hood.
Single exhaust stack is typical near cab and offset to the left.
S-2s and S-4s have a bigger turbocharger stack. Frame is simple,
regular platform.

 The S-2 was Alco's best-selling diesel locomotive and is still
seen today in freight yards, hauling freight on shortlines, and in
private industrial use. The S-1 is a less powerful but otherwise
similar design with a smaller, vertical radiator shutter area (leaving room for an extra access door). The S-2 shutters evolved
from panels of vertical slats to larger horizontal ones and then
to vertical again, a remarkably minor adjustment considering
the long production period. The S-3 and S-4 were respectively
S-1s and S-2s equipped with AAR trucks rather than with the
earlier Blunt trucks.

Alco S-6, T-6

Length: 45 ft. 6 in. *Horsepower:* S-6 900; T-6 1,000 *Cyl.:* 6
Date of mfr.: S-6 1955–1960; T-6 1958–1969 *Approx. no.
built:* S-6 126; T-6 57

The S-6 has a high cab with rounded windows over the hood.
Turbocharger stack is located forward on hood and centered.
The hood is nearly flat with a small lip over the headlight.
Square radiator shutters protrude from the flat nose. The single
exhaust fan is flush mounted in the top of the hood.

 The T-6 ("T" is for *Transfer*) uses the signature sculptured
nose from Alco road diesels. Radiator shutters have moved to
the side and a large round exhaust fan housing sits atop the
hood at the front. As is typical with older locomotives, vents
and louvers are now quite variable.

 These two locomotives are quite similar and use the same
platform as earlier Alco switchers. As with the S-1 and S-2, Alco
seems to have found a good design and stuck with it. Minor
variations do occur. For example, some models were built with a
lower cab to clear obstructions. The S-5 was the predecessor to
this line and was outwardly identical but had only 800 horsepower. Just seven were built in 1954, and apparently none survive.

END-CAB SWITCHERS

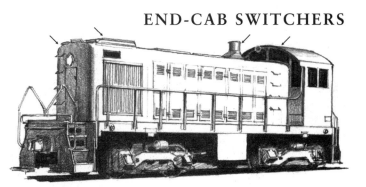

Alco S-1, S-3

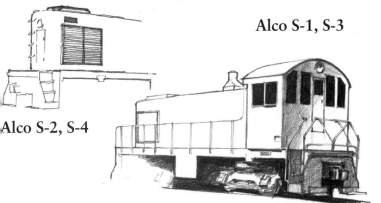

Alco S-2, S-4

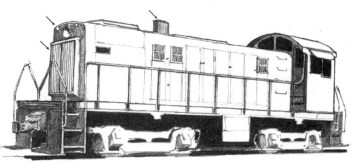

Alco S-6

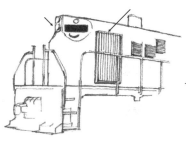

Alco T-6

MLW S-13

Length: 45 ft. 6 in. *Horsepower:* 1,000 *Cyl.:* 6
Date of mfr.: 1959–1967 *Approx. no. built:* 56

Similar to an Alco S-6 but even rarer. Sits particularly high on its Alco-type trucks. Oblong turbocharger stack is toward the front of the hood. Front of hood is flat with projecting radiator shutters. Number boards are above the shutters on angled mountings. Walkways step down toward the front.

While Alco was building the S-6, Montreal Locomotive Works, an Alco affiliate at the time, produced their S-13, a very few of which survive in far corners of Canada. Developed from the now almost nonexistent S-11 and the nonexistent S-12, it was far more successful. Should you happen across an S-11, note that it was not turbocharged and has a small round exhaust stack back near the cab. The S-12 had a turbocharger with its oblong stack also near the cab, unlike the S-13.

Baldwin VO 1000, DS-4-4-10, S-12

Length: 48 ft. 10 in. *Horsepower:* 1,000 (S-12 was 1,200)
Cyl.: 8 (6 or 8 in DS-4-4-10 and S-12) *Date of mfr.:* 1936–1956
Approx. no. built: 1,500

Long hood with typical Baldwin headlight fairing. Short, stubby cab makes locomotive appear larger than it is. Handrail is hood mounted. May have one exhaust stack centered in front of cab or four spaced along hood offset to the left. Cab typically has high windows over the hood.

Although rare, these locomotives can be seen regularly in the South and in California on smaller local railroads. They are essentially the same machine, but in three different styles used over the years. The early VO 1000s sported a pointed nose with distinctive round grille and side radiators, a real collector's item to discover. By 1941, the nose was still pointed but less so, and the front grille was now rectangular without side radiators. The curved detailing at the steps was retained for a while. In 1946, the VO 1000 was relabeled DS-4-4-10 and the nose was flattened. Finally, in 1951 it became the more powerful S-12. It should be noted that this line was accompanied by a smaller locomotive, the VO 660 of which there are so few, if any, examples that it rates only this mention. The VO 660 evolved into the DS-4-4-6 and the S-8 with superficial design changes similar to those of its big brother.

END-CAB SWITCHERS

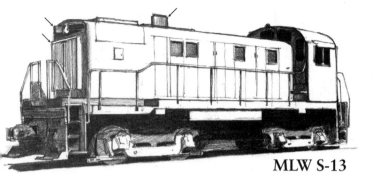

MLW S-13

Baldwin VO 1000

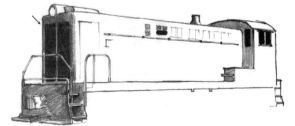

Baldwin DS-4-4-10, S-12

EMD Early Switcher Genealogy

To comprehend EMD's baffling array of model numbers, it is useful to retrace the evolution of their diesel prime mover development that began in 1936. Using the Winton 201-A diesel engine, a two-cycle V8, and built on the 44-ft.-5-in.-long platform, diesel switchers were offered in two versions, the SC and the SW. The "C" and "W" stand for *cast* or *welded* frame while the "S" appears to have been the initial for *six hundred,* the horsepower rating. These were the first of EMD's mass-produced locomotives and forerunners of a line of similar diesel switchers that led to EMD's domination of the market through the '50s, '60s, and '70s. A very few of the 119 built by 1939 remain in industrial service today, but none with railroads.

In 1937 a more powerful model was added using a 12-cylinder version of the Winton engine. The "N" series, presumably for *nine-hundred* horsepower, was also available in cast or welded frame as the NC and NW. Variation in electrical equipment and other detail resulted in the NC1, NC2, NW1, and NW4. Relatively few were built, and there appear to be no survivors.

All these models were succeeded in 1939 by the SW1 and the NW2 using EMD's new 567 diesel engine (six and twelve cylinders respectively) on the standard 44-ft.-5-in. frame. The 600-horsepower SW1 remained in the catalog until 1953, and a few are in service today doing light duty at local industries and on branch lines. The 1,000-horsepower NW2 (the terminology begins to slip) became EMD's biggest seller ever by 1949, and dozens are still in use. To be thorough, it should be noted that in 1942 seven stretched NW2s were built, called NW3s. In 1947, thirteen more were lengthened, this time by adding a rear hood, and called NW5s. A few remain in use. Some sources classify these models as road switchers.

In 1949 it was decided, presumably at high levels, that "SW" meant *switcher* and the NW2, raised to 1,200 horsepower, became the SW7 and in 1950 the SW9. In 1954 another change in model number philosophy, that they should reflect horsepower, resulted in the SW1200, the culmination of the NW2, that sold until 1966. All these twin-exhaust-stack locomotives are nearly indistinguishable and represent a single design that sold well over 3,000 units.

Along the way *cow-and-calf* teams of switchers, with only the cow having a cab, were devised for transferring trains or parts of trains from one area to another. Called *transfer* locomotives, they have largely disappeared, replaced by road switchers. A very few of those created from NW2s (TR2) and SW7s (TR4) have lately worked the Chicago Belt railway.

Alas, there is room for further confusion. Back in 1950, EMD, still interested in the smaller-engined locomotive market, introduced an eight-cylinder, 800-horsepower locomotive, the SW8, which, in 1954 "split" into the SW600 and SW900 of six and eight cylinders respectively and horsepower as per their model numbers under the latest system. The SW600 was not popular, and only a few sold before 1962 when it was dropped. The SW900 continued with more success until 1965. These three single-stack locomotives are virtually identical externally.

Clearing the boards, the SW1000 and SW1500 with the new 645 engine appeared in 1966, replacing all the earlier 567 powered switchers. Somewhat different in appearance, with a taller cab, they were still built on the short frame. The tall cab was a problem for a yard switcher, and a variant, the SW1001, with lower cab was offered. The SW1500 was intended for road switcher duty as well as yard work and although popular was limited by its short frame and too little space for the preferred road-going Blomberg trucks. Flexicoil trucks and larger fuel tanks were fitted to most SW1500s, but the design problem remained, to be finally resolved in 1974 with the introduction of the lengthened MP15 locomotive series.

An order of 60 "stretch" SW1500s built in 1973 for National Railways of Mexico, called SW1504s, appears to have provided the inspiration for the MP15 locomotive seven years later ("MP" means *multipurpose* while "15" is presumably short for *1,500 horsepower*. Here we go again). Still using the 12-cylinder 567 engine, the MP15, with its AC-powered cousin and the more economical eight-cylinder MP15T, brought to a close EMD's long saga of diesel-switcher design.

Making sense of EMD's switch engine genealogy involves comprehending more model numbers than models. Although this book is about the visual aspect of train spotting, an understanding of engine development and related nomenclature is necessary to grasp the seemingly aimless proliferation of similar diesel locomotives.

EMD SW1

Length: 44 ft. 5 in. *Horsepower:* 600 *Cyl.:* 6
Date of mfr.: 1939–1953 *Approx. no. built:* 660

Short hood with pronounced notch ahead of cab. Single exhaust stack. Radiator grille on flat nose over large sandbox that is diagnostic. Hood-mounted handrail. Radiator fan is flush mounted in top of hood.

This compact, versatile locomotive has found work on shortlines and switching yards for half a century. As more powerful locomotives displaced it over the years, it was relegated to lighter tasks and can be found occasionally throughout the U.S. on small railroads and local industries. The short hood is centered on the platform, giving it a balanced look and a pleasant character with its generous platforms, front and rear. Later models had a straight taper from the top of the hood to the cab rather than the two-stage notch. Front top cab windows may be squared off.

EMD NW2

Length: 44 ft. 5 in. *Horsepower:* 1,000 *Cyl.:* 12
Date of mfr.: 1939 –1949 *Approx. no. built:* 143

High cab accentuated by hood notch. Notch becomes single taper in later models. Large windows at cab front. Side windows vary. Flat nose with partial radiator grille is diagnostic. Two exhaust stacks. Early models had no louvers in hood, most probably have some by now. Note frame profile with fairing leading to steps. Cylindrical fuel tank. AAR trucks.

EMD's best seller despite the war years of suspended production. With the NW2, EMD consolidated the manufacturing activities of chassis, engine, and electrical components in-house.

The very rare NW5 is similar but was lengthened to provide for a short hood containing a steam generator for passenger train use.

END-CAB SWITCHERS

EMD SW1

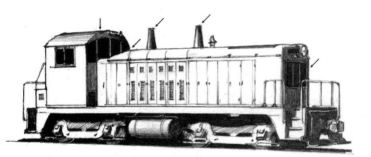

EMD NW2

EMD NW5

EMD SW7, SW9, SW1200

Length: 44 ft. 5 in. *Horsepower:* 1,200 *Cyl.:* 12
Date of mfr.: SW7 1949–1951; SW9 1951–1953;
SW1200 1954–1956 *Approx. no. built:* SW7 493; SW9 815;
SW1200 1024

Two conical exhaust stacks indicate 12-cylinder engine. Flat nose with full-height radiator shutters. Radiator is flush mounted in hood top. Twin over-and-under headlight assembly with angled number boards. Cylindrical fuel tanks.

These three are indistinguishable but for some louver placements. Hood louvers will vary, but SW7 originally had full-height louvers with a horizontal strip left out for lettering. The SW9 and SW1200 had louvers only to belt high. Some determined spotters will count battery box louvers; the SW1200 went to five after SW9's six, but this is unreliable, particularly after 40 years. A variant in Canada is the SW1200RS, which has a hooded headlight assembly with large number boards.

Cow-and-calf transfer versions of the SW7 and SW9 are still in use as the TR4 and TR5 respectively.

EMD SW8, SW600, SW900

Length: 44 ft. 5 in. *Horsepower:* SW8 800; SW600 600;
SW900 900 *Cyl.:* SW8, SW900 8; SW600 6
Date of mfr.: 1950–1965 *Approx. no. built:* 743

A series of nearly identical switchers on standard 1936 EMD platform. Similar to SW7, 9, and 1200 but with single exhaust stack. Typical EMD hood taper. Flat front with full-height radiator shutters and projecting headlight housing with integral number boards. Front cab windows are rectangular. Two side windows. Cylindrical fuel tank. Original handrails were mounted on hood sides. AAR trucks.

END-CAB SWITCHERS

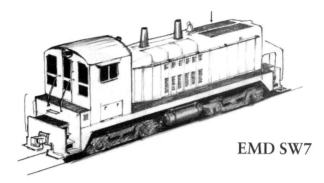

EMD SW7

EMD SW9, SW1200

EMD TR5 Cow and Calf, TR4

EMD SW1000, SW1001, SW1500

Length: 44 ft. 8 in. *Horsepower:* SW1000 (SW1001) 1,000;
SW1500 1,500 *Cyl.:* SW1000 8; SW1500 12
Date of mfr.: 1966–1974 (SW1001 to 1986) *Approx. no. built:*
SW1000 118; SW1001 151; SW1500 807

Long hood with particularly tall cab and four side windows.
Typical EMD taper from hood to cab. Headlight and number
board housing protrudes over flat nose with radiator shutters.
May have full-frame-mounted handrail with stanchions or minimal hood-mounted type. Single exhaust stack is SW1000 or
1001, twin stacks are SW1500s. Oddly beveled battery boxes at
rear of cab. Most have short, rounded fuel tank with air reservoir. The SW1001 is an SW1000 with a lower cab for clearing
obstacles.

   This model was the successor to the SW900 and SW1200 series, differing visually with the extra-tall cab, headlight housing,
and radiator treatment. The radiator opening on top of the
hood wrapped around the sides and was noticeably longer on
the SW1500, reaching over the sand fillers. Many SW1500s
were equipped with Flexicoil trucks for greater speed on road-
switching duties, although AAR trucks were standard. However,
the relatively short chassis couldn't accommodate the favored
Blomberg trucks, and this series was eventually succeeded by the
longer MP15. Still, hundreds remain in service in the U.S. on
large and small carriers.

EMD SW1504

Length: 46 ft. 8 in. *Horsepower:* 1,000 *Date of mfr.:* 1973
Approx. no. built: 60

Only seen in Mexico, the SW1504 is visually a lengthened
SW1500 with Blomberg trucks. Boxy, louvered air-filter housing
just ahead of cab. Two exhaust stacks. Flat nose with projecting
radiator grille. Prominent headlight number-board assembly.
Eight handrail stanchions, one more than SW1500. Rounded
EMD profile fuel tank with air reservoir. Note expanded sand
boxes.

END-CAB SWITCHERS

EMD SW 1000, SW1500

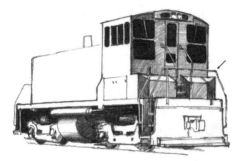

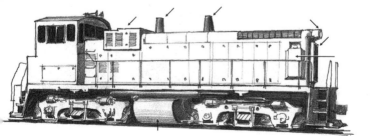

EMD SW1504

EMD MP15(DC), MP15AC, MP15T

Length: MP15 47 ft. 8 in.–48 ft. 8 in.; MP15AC 49 ft. 2 in.;
MP15T 50 ft. 2 in. *Horsepower:* 1,500 *Cyl.:* MP15, MP15AC
12; MP15T *Cyl.:* 8 *Date of mfr.:* 1974–1987
Approx. no. built: 505

MP15(DC) closely resembles a stretched SW1500 with
Blomberg trucks and rounded fuel tank with air reservoir. Most
have squared-off filter housing just ahead of cab, which is likely
to be beveled at rear. Earlier models may have narrower steps.
Radiator enclosure in top of hood wraps around hood sides.
Two exhaust stacks may be in a silencer box. May have expanded sand boxes.

MP15AC is generally similar but with plain, flat nose and radiator air intakes on hood sides, forward and low. Radiator assembly projects above top of hood. Noticeably longer fuel tank.
New step design.

MP15T is longer still but with side air intakes and radiators
as on MP15AC. Also has new-style steps. Note turbocharger
stack and right-side-only blower duct. Headlight number-board
housing is bulkier.

The last of EMD's yard switchers, the MP15 is actually a
dual-purpose locomotive able to function as a road switcher as
well. The original MP15 was renamed MP15DC when the AC
version appeared. The MP15T, though longer, is intended as a
fuel-efficient version with a turbocharged eight-cylinder engine.
The entire order, save one, of 42 locomotives went to Seaboard
System in 1984 and 1985 and are now operated by CSX.

Fairbanks-Morse H-12-44

Length: 48 ft. 10 in. *Horsepower:* 1,200 *Cyl.:* 6 *Date of mfr.:*
1950–1961 *Approx. no. built:* 335

Quite variable but the H-12-44 is the only end-cab switcher in
this book with a hood as tall as the cab. Originally fitted with a
body and cab designed by Raymond Loewy (as was its predecessor, the H-10-44), the styling features were dropped one by one
until it became a very straightforward-looking little locomotive.

Until 1952 the nose was sloped and the walkway steps swept
up to the cab in a curved fairing. The cab roof was rounded and
had an extended awning to the rear. Later models straightened
the nose, squared off the cab and battery boxes, and chopped
off the rear overhang. Practicality laid waste to Loewy's design
in 1956 when the last H-12-44s were shortened by 3 ft., giving
them the stubby appearance of a children's book illustration.

END-CAB SWITCHERS

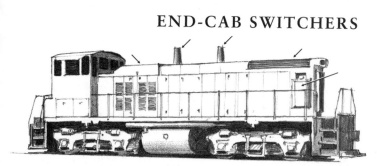

EMD MP15(DC)

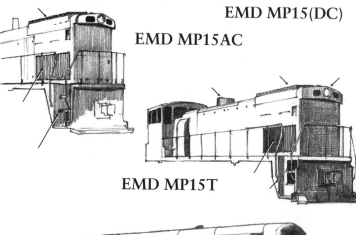

EMD MP15AC

EMD MP15T

Late

FM H-12-44

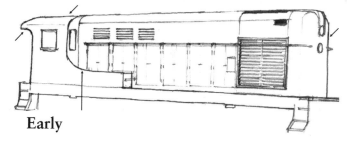

Early

19

Alco RS1

Length: 54 ft. 11¾ in. *Horsepower:* 1,000 *Cyl.:* 6
Date of mfr.: 1941–1960 *Approx. no. built:* 417

Long low hood with square radiator fan housing. Radiator shutters at each side of hood are well forward. Rounded cab roof. Large windows front, rear, and sides. Flat ends with recessed headlight. Number boards on hood sides. Short hood is same height. Late models have a crisp edge to the top of the nose, front, and rear. Large single stack is offset to the left (long hood is usually forward). Flat oval fuel tank and battery box are hung below frame. AAR trucks.

Alco's straightforward classification system leaves no doubt that the RS1 is their first road switcher, basically an S2 (see page 6) lengthened to provide room for a steam generator in the short hood for the Rock Island Railroad. It is distinguished from later descendants by its less-rounded corners and extended cab roof, front and rear, and radiator-fan housing. Many were requisitioned during World War II for sevice in Iran and Russia as well as the U.S. military. The RSD1 is a C-C, six-axle version with unequally spaced wheels and can still be found in industrial use. Ex-army RSD1s may show a noticeably lower cab roof.

Alco RS2, RS3

Length: 55 ft. 11¾ in. *Horsepower:* RS2 1,500–1,600;
RS3 1,600 *Cyl.:* 12 *Date of mfr:* RS2 1946–1950;
RS3 1950–1956 *Approx. no. built:* RS2 383; RS3 1,370

Long, low hood with pronounced rounding at the corners, including the cab. Round radiator-fan housing. Large square area of nearly full-height radiator shutters on each side of hood. Single turbocharger stack toward nose is offset to the left. Later models had stack centered and mounted crosswise. RS2 has the batteries in a box under the frame, and fuel tank above the platform under the cab floor, leaving a large space between the trucks. The RS3 has battery boxes on the short-hood walkways and fuel tanks hung from the frame.

These are the familiar and much admired Alcos so often referred to with affection even as their numbers diminish. A versatile locomotive designed for passenger as well as freight use, they shared mechanical components with their streamlined FA and PA contemporaries. Their flexibility and reliability have kept them in demand for shortline work even today, and some smaller railroads use them as their primary motive power.

The RSC2 and RSC3 were six-wheel A1A truck versions that have apparently disappeared. Their successors, the RSD4 and RSD5 six-wheel C-C models are also virtually extinct on railroad rosters.

ROAD SWITCHERS/LOW HOOD

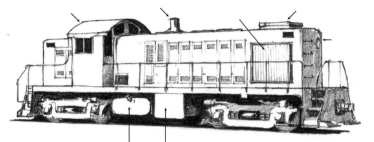

Alco RS1

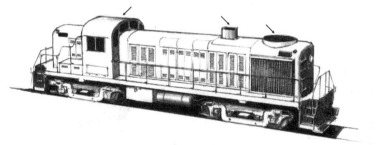

Alco RS3

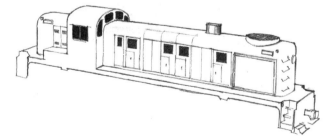

EMD RS1325

Length: 52 ft. 2 in. *Horsepower:* 1,325 *Cyl.:* 12
Date of mfr.: 1960 *Approx. no. built:* 2

Unusual low-sloping hood opposite long hood. Short hood is the front. Long hood is similar to SW1200 (see page 14) but with longer notch. Two exhaust stacks. Flexicoil trucks and cylindrical fuel tank. Frame-mounted handrail.

An interesting if unsuccessful design intended to bring power to tight curves and light rail where standard road switchers are restricted. This locomotive is included here because, in spite of there being only a pair in existence, they are likely to be seen by many. Until sold or retired, they can be spotted between Peoria and Taylorville on the Chicago and Illinois Midland Railway tracks.

EMD GMD1

Horsepower: 1,200 *Cyl.:* 12
Date of mfr.: 1958–1960 *Approx no. built:* 1001

Long flat hood with prominent headlight number-board assembly. Flat noses with louvered access doors in small hood. Two exhaust stacks. Rounded EMD-profile fuel tank. Flexicoil trucks. Hood ventilation with louvers only. No battery boxes on walkway. Handrail may be hood mounted.

Seen in Canada only. Some originally sold with C-C trucks; Canadian National rebuilt them with B-B flexicoils.

ROAD SWITCHERS/LOW HOOD

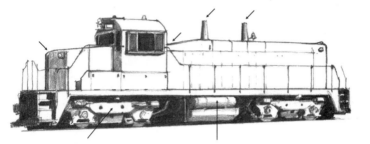

EMD RS1325

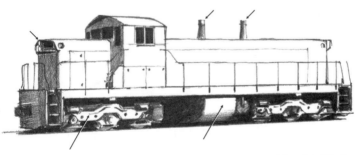

EMD GMD1

Morrison Knudsen MK1200G

Length: 56 ft. 2 in. *Horsepower:* 1,200 *Cyl.:* 16
Date of mfr.: 1994 *Approx. no. built:* 4

Short, stubby, sloping low hood. Tall cab with large windshield, windows. Long hood with various air intakes and two round exhaust fans on top. Frame-mounted handrails. Long cylindrical fuel tanks. Standard Blomberg trucks.

Unusual first design from a new locomotive manufacturer (MK Rail has long experience in rebuilding locomotives of all types). Powered with natural gas, the MK1200G is intended for switching work in dense urban areas of high air pollution and tough exhaust restrictions. Two each have been leased by the Santa Fe and Union Pacific railroads and are in service in the Los Angeles area. The prime mover is a Caterpillar diesel that produces a particularly low level of pollutants and has a low profile permitting a lower long hood and better visibility. Union Pacific has reportedly requested that its pair of MK1200Gs be equipped to operate long hood forward.

Baldwin Road Switcher Series

Length: 58 ft. *Horsepower:* 1,500–1,600 *Cyl.:* 8
Date of mfr.: 1946–1955 *Approx. no. built:* 397

Long flat hood laced with louvers. Turbocharger bulge on left side only is diagnostic. Single tubocharger stack is offset to the left. Forward side radiator air intakes vary — some low, some mid-height. Radiator is top-mounted over intakes. Flat nose with recessed headlight. Number boards are variable. Cylindrical fuel tank.

These locomotives somewhat resemble the Alcos with their long hood and high cab, but the hood is higher and less rounded in character. Field marks such as frame profile and air intakes are unreliable. It is very unlikely that you will discover a Baldwin road switcher operating anywhere, but there are a treasured few out there, and after mastering the Baldwin numbering system I wanted to share it.

> The B-B model with AAR-type trucks was originally the DRS-4-4-15.
> The A1A model (equally spaced wheels) was the DRS-6-4-15.
> The C-C model (unequally spaced wheels) was the DRS-6-6-15.

Something like "Diesel road switcher - number of truck wheels - number of driving wheels - horsepower divided by 100."

Then in 1950, with a horsepower increase to 1,600,

> The DRS-4-4-15 became the AS-16
> The DRS-6-4-15 became the AS-416
> The DRS-6-6-15 became the AS-616

All this may be elementary to the Baldwin fans out there, but to someone just happening along it can be intimidating.

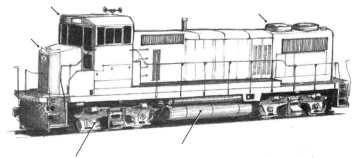

MK1200G

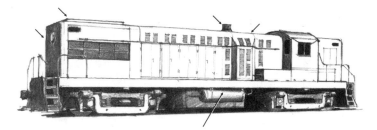

Baldwin DRS-4-4-15

Alco RS11

Length: 57 ft. 2½ in. *Horsepower:* 1,800 *Cyl.:* 12
Date of mfr.: 1956–1964 *Approx. no. built:* 426

Long high hood deeply notched at the corners. Notched nose may be high or low with two-piece windshield over it. Large square radiator grilles and single round radiator fan on top. Long battery boxes on walkway ahead of hood on both sides. Long hood shows a row of three or five square car body filters on each side. Simple uninterrupted frame profile. Eight handrail stanchions.

Alco's first higher-horsepower road switcher, the RS11 is still seen daily with dozens in service on shortline railroads. Short high-hood version gives a completely different character, but Alco notches are consistent clues. AAR trucks, hood notches on long low hood, and single round roof fan describe an RS11. Montreal Locomotive Works built identical units lacking the notches, but they are no longer in use.

Successors to the RS11, the RS32 and RS36 are extremely rare and indistinguishable from each other except that all RS32s were low nosed. Few were built, and fewer than a dozen remain. Similar to RS11 but with hood filters grouped along sides. The RS32 added 200 horsepower with a newer engine. The RS36 used the RS11's 1,800-horsepower engine.

A nearly extinct variant, the RS27 was an RS11 with the cab pushed forward to make room for a 16-cylinder engine. Only 27 were built, but they were important as the forerunner of the coming Century series.

Alco C-420

Length: 60 ft. 3 in. *Horsepower:* 2,000 *Cyl.:* 12
Date of mfr.: 1963–1968 *Approx. no. built:* 131

Long hood has flush-mounted radiator shutters low on the sides to the rear. Alco notched corners are milder. Low nose is long and without notches. A very few had high, notched noses with steam generators. Cab is uniquely pointed as is the two-piece windshield. May have optional cylindrical fuel tanks.

"C" usually denotes six-wheel truck locomotives, but in this case it stands for Alco's new (in 1963) Century series, with the "4" in 420 relating to four-wheel B-B trucks and the number "20," the horsepower divided by 100. Lightest of the Century locomotives, the C-420 competed directly with EMD's GP30 and General Electric's U25B with some success. At this writing the three or four dozen survivors are well scattered across the U.S., Canada, and Mexico.

ROAD SWITCHERS/HIGH HOOD/B-B

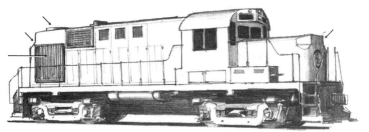

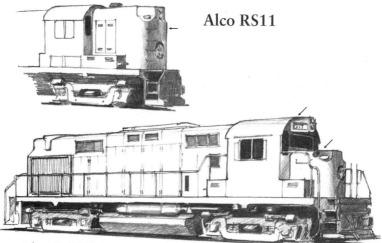

Alco RS11

Alco RS27

Alco RS32, RS36

Alco C-420

EMD GP7

Length: 55 ft. 11 in. *Horsepower:* 1,500 *Cyl.:* 16
Date of mfr.: 1949–1954 *Approx. no. built:* 2,610

The classic diesel road switcher configuration; high long and
short hoods and with cab set back from front (or rear as the
case may be). Four cooling fans paired front and rear atop long
hood. Two exhaust stacks. Frame profile has a deep center section over EMD-type rounded fuel tank. Dynamic brakes may be
present with bulging blister midway along hood and with a
large additional cooling fan.

Although late getting to the market with a true road switcher,
EMD certainly came up with a successful one with the "General
Purpose" GP7. It is often credited with completing the dieseliza-
tion of American railroads. After stumbling with the BL2 (see
page 104), EMD combined the reliable F-series machinery with
the maintenance advantages of a hood-type superstructure and
proceeded, with the later GP9 (see below), to outsell the combined competitors two to one through the '50s. "Geeps" are
commonly seen today, although most have been rebuilt at some
time or another, disturbing spotters' details.

EMD GP9

Length: 56 ft. 2 in. *Horsepower:* 1,750 *Cyl.:* 16
Date of mfr.: 1954–1959 *Approx. no. built:* 3,436

Successor to the GP7, the GP9 is nearly identical, and spotting
tips noted above should apply. Later models did replace the four
round cooling fans with two larger ones at each end of the
hood, and the side skirt over the fuel tank was cut away. A few
were built with a low nose, a hint of things to come. Some
sources describe a different louver layout for the GP9 with fewer
under the radiators and new rows of louvers amidships on the
hood. Also, the GP9 reportedly lacks most, if not all, louvers
under the cab. How reliable these distinctions are after 40 years
of heavy use and refurbishing is a further challenge to the spotter. The GP9 may or may not have dynamic brakes. GP10s and
GP11s are Illinois Central rebuilds of GP9s.

EMD GP18

Length: 56 ft. 2 in. *Horsepower:* 1,800 *Cyl.:* 16
Date of mfr.: 1959–1963 *Approx. no. built:* 350

Last of the original line of "Geeps," the GP18 shows only subtle
changes, including relating model number to horsepower. The
high air intakes, front and rear, had a horizontal grid over the
radiator shutters rather than the original chicken wire. The deep
section of the frame profile is often cut away.

ROAD SWITCHERS/HIGH HOOD/B-B

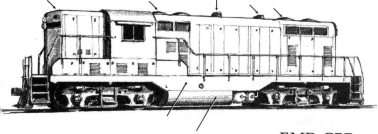

EMD GP7

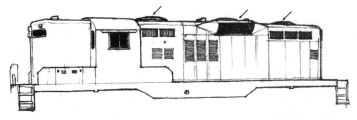

EMD GP9

EMD GP18

EMD GP20

Length: 56 ft. 2 in. *Horsepower:* 2,000 *Cyl.:* 16
Date of mfr.: 1959–1962 *Approx. no. built:* 260

Similar to the GP18 but with a single turbocharger stack and three radiator fans — two large fans at either end of the hood and a smaller one just ahead of the rear fan. Positive identification is made by the louvered, rectangular boxes on each side of the hood just behind the cab at the tubocharger air intake. Flat one-piece windshield. Note frame skirt is cut away to make room for air reservoirs. Almost all GP20s were low nosed, and most had dynamic brakes.

Despite potential maintenance problems, turbocharging seemed a likely way to increase horsepower for the western railroads that were demanding it. Union Pacific installed turbochargers on GP9s to test the concept, and EMD followed with their own conversions and then with the GP20, which is essentially a turbocharged GP18. Much was made of the claim that three GP20s could substitute for four F units. Although not many were sold, turbocharging went on to become commonplace on road switchers during the '60s.

EMD GP15-1 (GP15T)

Length: 54 ft. 11 in. *Horsepower:* 1,500 *Cyl.:* 12
(GP15T, 8 cyl.) *Date of mfr.:* 1976–1982 (GP15T, 1982–1983)
Approx. no. built: 340 (GP15T, 28)

A short, clean-lined "Geep"-looking locomotive (note short fuel tank) with EMD's flat-topped, pointed nose and angled cab roof. Radiator air intakes are low at the rear of the high hood, and radiators are mounted on top in a GE-like housing. The frame profile is cut out for the air reservoirs. The hood section just behind the cab varies, with some models having many louvers, the others with a typical rectangular, inertial air-filter housing. On those units with the filter housing, the duct is much larger. The duct continues horizontally along the walkway, causing a step at the rear truck. There are nine handrail stanchions. Unless modified, there are two exhaust stacks.

The GP15T differs with its turbocharged eight-cylinder engine, intended to be more fuel efficient. The exhaust silencer is mounted just aft of the equipment-blower section and the radiator air intakes are larger. Dynamic brakes were offered on all models, but only the CSX GP15Ts are so equipped.

Designed to compete with the railroads' plans to rebuild older locomotives needed for lighter work, the GP15 series was not particularly successful. Still, nearly all are in daily use with major railroads such as Union Pacific, CSX, and Conrail.

ROAD SWITCHERS/HIGH HOOD/B-B

EMD GP20

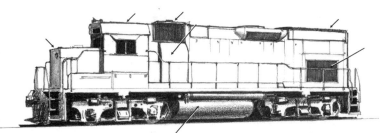

EMD GP15-1

EMD GP30

Length: 56 ft. 2 in. *Horsepower:* 2,250 *Cyl.:* 16
Date of mfr.: 1961–1963 *Approx. no. built:* 906

Unmistakable. High roof fairing runs from cab roof past dynamic-brake blister whether or not the locomotive was so equipped. Cab is slightly pointed with a two-piece windshield. Cab eaves are noticeably rounded. Low nose was typical, but 160 or so peculiar-looking high-nosed models were built, most running short hood forward. A few were sold on AAR trucks, but Blombergs were standard. Two large radiator cooling fans on each side of a smaller one are at the end of the long hood. The walkway is raised on both sides to provide a pipe and electrical run on the left and a blower duct on the right. Frame profile is distinctive and shared with the GP35.

EMD abandoned their quick trial at relating the model number to the horsepower with the GP30. "Thirty" must have just sounded better when competing with GE's U25B. Perhaps the competition also resulted in an attempt to style the locomotive by tidying up the roof and rounding some hard edges. Opinion varies as to the success of the design. In any case, it was not carried on to any other EMD models — probably a story there somewhere. Better than a third of the GP30 production is still working around the country.

EMD GP35

Length: 56 ft. 2 in. *Horsepower:* 2,500 *Cyl.:* 16
Date of mfr.: 1963–1966 *Approx. no. built:* 1,333

Typical EMD design. Long tall hood with radiator air intakes high to the rear and equipment air intakes high behind cab. Cab is flat roofed and flat fronted while low hood is pointed and flat topped. Note frame profile. Later models had an even thinner frame section above air reservoirs. Three radiator exhaust fans — two large with a small in between — in raised housings. Blower duct is on left walkway only. Fuel tanks are EMD's graceful rounded shape. Blomberg trucks. Single turbocharger stack. A few were high nosed.

Successor to the unusual-looking GP30, the GP35 reverted to more typical configuration and established EMD's hard-edged look down to the current GP60. Spotting from the GP35 on will essentially be observing variations on this theme. Hundreds are still in service on railroads large and small.

A very similar nonturbocharged model was the 1,800-horsepower GP28. Only 26 were built in 1964 and 1965. Possibly a dozen are still running, some in Mexico. They have only two cooling fans and two low exhaust stacks.

ROAD SWITCHERS/HIGH HOOD/B-B

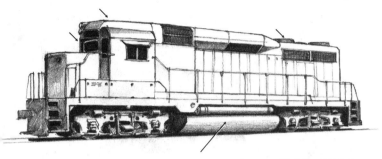

EMD GP30

EMD GP35

EMD GP38, GP38-2

Length: 59 ft. 2 in. *Horsepower:* 2,000 *Cyl.:* 16
Date of mfr.: GP38 1966–1971; GP38-2 1972–1984
Approx. no. built: GP38 730; GP38-2 2188

Classic EMD configuration. Note the two radiator cooling fans and the two exhaust stacks. Traction-motor blower duct on left side (late GP38-2s may have newer type as shown on GP49 and GP50). Frame is cut out at air reservoir. The hood roof is getting lumpy with the equipment-blower housing, the paper air-filter box, and the dynamic-brake housing when present. Ten handrail stanchions.

An extremely successful design with the two models accounting for nearly 3,000 units sold. EMD correctly read the market in the mid-'60s and offered this versatile medium-horsepower locomotive that fit so many railroads' needs. Surprisingly few modifications were made over the eight-year production run, but some later GP38-2s had a 7-in.-longer nose (still on the 59-ft.-2-in. platform) and an anticlimber projecting out over the pilot (a way to walk around the longer nose). The difference between the two locomotives was in the electronics, the Dash-2 having a modular cabinet system for easier maintenance. This expressed itself externally with great subtlety; namely the famous "oblong water-level sight gauge" on the right-hand side back near the radiator, and the bolted, rather than hinged, battery box access doors.

EMD GP39, GP39-2

Length: 59 ft. 2 in. *Horsepower:* 2,300 *Cyl.:* 12
Date of mfr.: GP39 1969–1970; GP39-2 1974–1987
Approx. no. built: GP39 23; GP39-2 249

GP39s are nearly identical to GP38s but with a single turbocharger stack. Partway through the GP39-2 production, the radiator was reduced to one rectangle, shorter than the previous pair. At the same time the engine was moved back 3 ft. inside the hood, taking the dynamic-brake housing and traction blower duct with it. Note the resulting space aft of the cab. The last units built expanded the radiators again and switched to the new-type blower duct used on the GP49.

As an alternate to 16-cylinder power, EMD offered this turbocharged 12-cylinder model. It was not well received at the time, railroads fearing costly turbocharger maintenance. However in the '70s, with fuel costs becoming a major issue, the model was revived as the GP39-2. Its higher-altitude performance was also appreciated by roads crossing the Rockies. Fifteen GP49s were built that were 2,800-horsepower versions of the GP39 (to add to the confusion, the first six were originally called GP39Xs). They are replaced by the current GP59.

ROAD SWITCHERS/HIGH HOOD/B-B

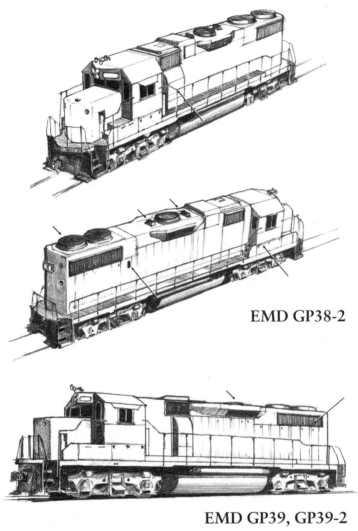

EMD GP38-2

EMD GP39, GP39-2

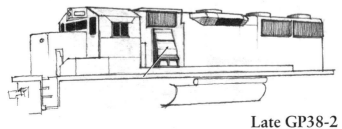

Late GP38-2

EMD GP40, GP40-2

Length: 59 ft. 2 in. *Horsepower:* 3,000 *Cyl.:* 16
Date of mfr.: GP40 1965–1971; GP40-2 1972–1986
Approx. no. built: GP40 1,243; GP40-2 1,121

Three large radiator fans and a turbocharger stack mark the
GP40 series, distinguishing it from its predecessor, the GP38 and
GP38-2. The locomotives are otherwise similar, with small detail
differences that occur on Dash-2 models: the water-level sight
gauge and the bolted, rather than hinged, battery boxes. Along
the way GP40-2s acquired Q-type radiator fans (quieter and
taller) and surface-mounted radiator intake grilles among other
updates, but these are not reliable identifiers. Radiator grilles are
noticeably smaller than the succeeding GP50 and GP60. The
GP40-2 marked the decline of interest in four-axle, high-pow-
ered locomotives that continues today as six-axle models heavily
outsell them.

Some interesting variations did occur. More than 200 wide-
nosed Comfort Cab GP40-2Ws were built for Canadian National Railways (see page 74) using the standard Canadian cab
design. Thirteen GP40Ps pull commuter trains for New Jersey
Transit. They are 3½ ft. longer at the rear with space for a steam
generator or head-end power equipment. The 1-ft.-longer
GP40X is notable for its angled radiator air intakes. It also has
elevated walkways on both sides and a distinctly pointed rear
nose. Only 23 were built, but all were bought by big railroads to
try out an improved adhesion system. All are thought to be operating on Santa Fe, Union Pacific, Southern Pacific, and Norfolk Southern (whose units may be running backward as they
were ordered high-nose, long hood forward by original owner
Southern Railway). GP40Xs are collector's items for spotters.

At this point in the evolution of EMD diesels, it becomes in-
creasingly difficult to tell the various types from each other. A
design plateau has been reached with a configuration that seems
able to contain the differences in the models offered from the
GP38 on up to the GP60. There may be just one 59-ft.-2-in. locomotive here with a narrow choice of prime movers and electronics. Some detail variation does occur but usually within a
production run resulting in what modelers refer to as *phases* of
a particular type. Manufacturers and railroads usually make no
phase distinctions in their nomenclature. A few specially designed versions for specific owners for certain uses occasionally
break up the pattern, but they are usually few in number and
thus rarely seen outside their areas.

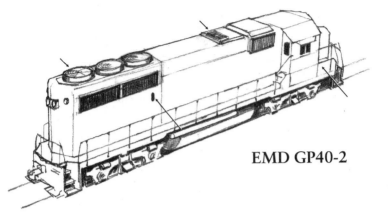

EMD GP40-2

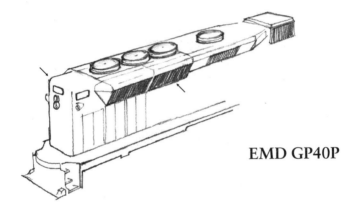

EMD GP40P

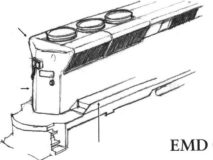

EMD GP40X

EMD GP50, GP59, GP60

Length: 59 ft. 2 in. *Horsepower:* GP50 3,500; GP59 3,000;
GP60 3,800 *Cyl.:* GP50, GP60 16; GP59 12 *Date of
mfr.:* GP50 1980–1985; GP59 1985–1989; GP60 1985–present
Approx no. built: GP50 275; GP59 36; GP60 350+

Visually, three nearly identical locomotives. Bodywise, all are
descended from the late GP38-2 with the slightly longer nose
and anticlimb front deck. They are distinguished from the earlier GP38 and GP39 series by their longer radiator grilles. All
have three radiator cooling fans and a low turbocharger silencer.
Dynamic-brake blisters vary considerably but become more
boxy on later models. Frame profiles are inconsistent with
GP50s, showing both the cutaway and simple straight type. All
the GP60s I have seen have only the straight version. After 1981
they had the new-type blower housing illustrated. As modelers
continue to focus on this series, more identifying details will
probably come to light.

GP59s are mechanical successors to the GP39 and GP49, as
EMD continued with its turbocharged 12-cylinder engine development. They are offered as lower-horsepower locomotives for
intermediate rather than high-speed service. Norfolk Southern
bought 35 of the production total. The basic chassis is also used
in the full-bodied F59PH, F69PH, and F59PHI commuter locomotives. See those entries.

The GP50 and GP60 are higher-horsepower versions of the
GP40-2, and thus head a long line of four-axle, 16-cylinder development. Santa Fe operates dozens of very handsome wide-
nosed GP60Ms (see page 76). EMD built three GP60 demonstrators with a softer look — rounded corners and a pointed
windshield — but it was too expensive to build and couldn't be
justified on aerodynamic grounds. Southern Railway was the
last to buy EMD high short hoods on their GP50s in 1980 and
1981.

EMD (AT&SF) CF7

Length: 55 ft. 11 in. *Horsepower:* 1,500 *Cyl.:* 16
Date of mfr.: 1970–1978 *Approx. no. built:* 233

Very stubby, sloped low nose with beveled corners. Extra-long
flat-faced cab and high EMD-style hood with high air intakes
fore and aft. Two round cooling fans at each end of hood. Two
or four exhaust stacks, usually four. Unusual, deep frame profile. Always rides on Blomberg trucks.

The result of a rebuild program carried out in the Santa Fe's
own shops, these unique F7A rebuilds are now scattered across
the country and can be seen regularly doing shortline work.
Most had a rounded roofline (as on the F7) but the last 50 or so
had a higher angled cab roof with room for air conditioning. Although details varied somewhat over the construction period,
the main field marks are consistent.

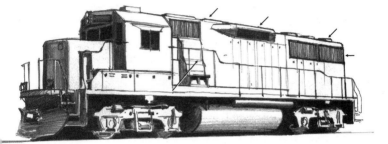

EMD GP50, GP60

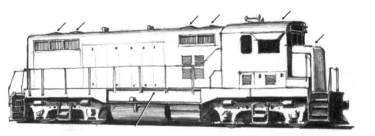

EMD (AT&SF) CF7

Alco C-424, C-425

Length: 59 ft. 4 in. *Horsepower:* C-424 2,400; C-425 2,500
Cyl.: 16 *Date of mfr.:* C-424 1963–1967; C-425 1964–1966
Approx. no. built: C-424 190; C-425 91

Short, blunt nose with the Century pointed cab and windshield.
Typical Alco rounded cab roof and cylindrical fuel tanks. Ten
handrail stanchions. Simple platform sits high on AAR trucks.
Three openings high on the hood with long roof hatch indicates
the presence of the optional dynamic-brake system. Hood ventilation opening is behind the cab.

A pair of very similar Century series locomotives. Most you
see will be C-424s. Distinguishing field marks are at the rear.
Early C-424s were unnotched and had a wider radiator housing
and a peculiar rear number-board arrangement as shown in the
accompanying sketches. When the C-425 arrived, both reverted
to notched corners (at the rear only), and the C-425 added a curiously shaped flat panel above the air-intake grille. The C-425
has a larger generator that accounts for the increased horsepower (and price).

Alco C-430

Length: 63 ft. 5 in. *Horsepower:* 3,000 *Cyl.:* 16
Date of mfr.: 1966–1968 *Approx. no. built:* 16

Similar to the preceding C-425, but more than 3 ft. longer. Af-
ter-cooler assembly is mounted high on hood behind cab and,
with B-B trucks, is diagnostic for the C-430. Trucks are the unusual Alco high-adhesion type found only on this model. (The
first two built had conventional AAR-type trucks.) Cylindrical
fuel tanks are mounted in pairs. The radiator area above the air
intake is slightly modified. Other details are typical Century series.

The C-430 was Alco's last attempt to compete with EMD and
GE in the four-axle road switcher market, and it had little suc-
cess. However, of the few built, several are still in regular use in
New Jersey and New York state.

ROAD SWITCHERS/HIGH HOOD/B-B

Early Alco C-424   Alco C-424   Alco C-425

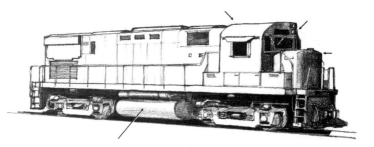

Alco C-425

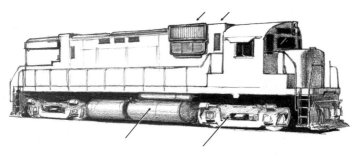

Alco C-430

GE U25B

Length: 60 ft. 2 in. *Horsepower:* 2,500 *Cyl.:* 16
Date of mfr.: 1959–1966 *Approx. no. built:* 478

Very clean long hood without bulges and bumps. Most had low nose, flat on top, with one-piece windshield. Large, screened radiator air intake is at rear of hood. There is a pronounced step in the walkways under the intakes. Cab roof is rounded and has additional side windows at each side of main window. Battery boxes are on right side of walkway fore and aft of the cab — a row of access doors is on the left walkway under the cab. Oval exhaust stack is mounted crosswise on hood. Radiator exhaust-fan grille is flush in hood top with raised center section. Angular fuel tanks.

The U25B was GE's entry into the road switcher market and was remarkably successful in taking over second place from struggling Alco within three years. Soon referred to as "U-boats," they became a common sight across the country through the '60s and '70s. "U" stands for Universal, "25" for the horsepower, and "B" for the four-axle version. A longer "C" model was also offered (see page 64). A few early models were sold with high noses, and later models had a two-piece windshield. The U25B was followed by the very similar U28B in 1966 (see below).

GE U28B

Length: 60 ft. 2 in. *Horsepower:* 2,800 *Cyl.:* 16
Date of mfr.: 1966 *Approx. no. built:* 148

Early models were indistinguishable from late U25Bs, while later ones were very similar to U30Bs with a snub-nosed appearance and a very short front hood. Hood air intakes are just behind the cab. Radiator housing projects out from hood over screen. Eight tall access doors on each side. Typical angular GE fuel tank. Long step in walkway at cab. Two additional side windows.

GE U30B

Length: 60 ft. 2 in. *Horsepower:* 3,000 *Cyl.:* 16
Date of mfr.: 1966–1975 *Approx. no. built:* 291

Continuation of the horsepower race on the same chassis. The early U30B can be identified by the smaller radiator screen and slight variation in the shape of the radiator assembly from the U28B's but lacks the widened rear hood section of the later U30B and U33B. This is pretty subtle in a 30-year-old locomotive that could well have been modified several times. Even the trucks may vary, as some locomotives were placed on trade-in EMD Blombergs, and a few were built with a high nose and operated long hood forward.

ROAD SWITCHERS/HIGH HOOD/B-B

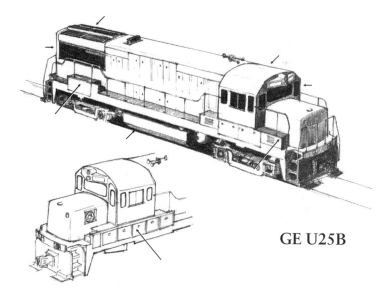

GE U25B

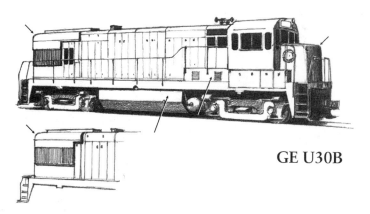

GE U30B

GE U28B

GE U33B

Length: 60 ft. 2 in. *Horsepower:* 3,300 *Cyl.:* 16
Date of mfr.: 1967–1970 *Approx. no. built:* 137

The U33B begins the spreading of the radiators, because of the increase in power, that continues to the present and has become a GE trademark. The whole radiator assembly, including the raised section, is now incorporated in a new housing over the widened hood, creating a verticle bump along the hood sides that will remain through the Dash-8 line. Other details remain similar to previous "U-boats."

GE U23B

Length: 60 ft. 2 in. *Horsepower:* 2,250 *Cyl.:* 12
Date of mfr.: 1968–1977 *Approx. no. built:* 425

One of GE's most successful moves was to introduce a less-powerful and cheaper-to-maintain model using a 12-cylinder version of their standard engine. According to some rosters, hundreds or nearly three-fourths of the original production are still in use. If so, they should be spotted everywhere and can be positively identified by counting the full-height access doors on each side. The U23B will have six rather than the eight on the other full-sized "U-boats" (the little eight-cylinder U18B has four such doors; see below). Counting access doors may seem an unexciting spotting exercise, but in the case of GE and their many model numbers for nearly the same locomotive, the alternative is to just be satisfied with "U-boat."

GE U36B

Length: 60 ft. 2 in. *Horsepower:* 3,600 *Cyl.:* 16
Date of mfr.: 1969–1974 *Approx. no. built:* 125

The last of the high-horsepower "U-boats," the U36B is virtually indistinguishable from the U33B, although some sources say it can be told from its predessessors by a subtle increase in the radiator wingspan. A sluggish market for high-horspower/high-maintenance locomotives plagued Alco and EMD as well as GE, and it would be three years before GE would introduce its four-axle Dash-7 line.

GE U18B

Length: 54 ft. 8 in. *Horsepower:* 1,800 *Cyl.:* 8
Date of mfr.: 1973–1976 *Approx. no. built:* 163

Visually, the U18B "Baby Boat" is a shortened U30B identifiable by its having only four tall engine access doors on each side of the hood. The fuel tank is also noticeably shorter, and it has only eight handrail stanchions aft of the cab.

ROAD SWITCHERS/HIGH HOOD/B-B

GE U33B

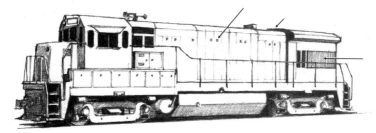

GE U36B

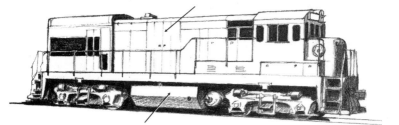

GE U18B

GE B23-7, BQ23-7

Length: 62 ft. 2 in. *Horsepower:* 2,250 *Cyl.:* 12
Date of mfr.: 1977–1984 *Approx. no. built:* 421

Close in appearance to the Universal series, the Dash-7 line is recognized by the distinct step in the hood forward of the radiators. The point where the hood widens is now just ahead of the exhaust stack and just behind the tall engine access doors. As is usual with GE, the number of engine access doors reflects the number of cylinders in the prime mover, six on each side. Although 2 ft. longer, the truck centers have remained the same, and it appears that space was added at the end platforms. Note the longer forward handrail and wider fairing where the platform meets the steps. Other details, such as cab, frame, and radiator housing, are consistent with earlier GE practice. Trucks vary from Blombergs to GE's own floating-bolster type. A few were built with a high nose and run backwards.

An interesting but homely variation was the BQ23-7, with its full-width Quarters Cab which anticipated the wide-cab designs now sweeping the locomotive industry. Intended to provide space for the conductor on cabooseless trains, only ten were built, as the caboose issue wasn't resolved at the time. Nine are still on CSX's roster at this writing.

GE B30-7, B36-7

Length: 62 ft. 2 in. *Horsepower:* B30-7 3,000; B36-7 3,600
Cyl.: 16 *Date of mfr.:* B30-7 1977–1981; B36-7 1980–1985
Approx. no. built: B30-7 199; B36-7 222

Similar to B23-7 but with eight full-height engine access doors indicating the presence of the 16-cylinder engine.

GE B30-7A, B30-7A1

Length: 62 ft. 2 in. *Horsepower:* 3,000 *Cyl.:* 12
Date of mfr.: B30-7A 58; B30-7A1 1982
Approx. no. built: B30-7A 58; B30-7A1 22

To complicate things a bit we have here a 12-cylinder version of the B30-7, resulting from an order of B23-7s being upgraded during manufacture to 3,000 horsepower. They are operated only by Union Pacific who, unfortunately for the train spotter, also runs B23-7s that are identical to the B30-7As. Only the roster numbers can help here.

A further aberration is the B30-7A1. Twenty-two high short-hood locomotives were built for the Southern Railway who liked to run long-hood forward. These units, now with Norfolk Southern, can be identified by an additional screened opening just forward of the cab. In addition, 119 cabless booster units were built for Burlington Northern.

GE B23-7, B30-7, B36-7

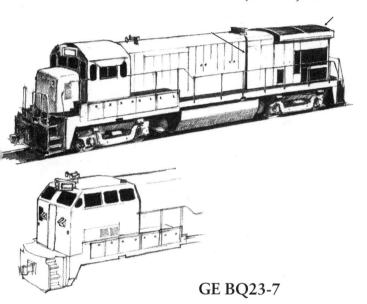

GE BQ23-7

GE B39-8

Length: 66 ft. 4 in. *Horsepower:* 3,900 *Cyl.:* 16
Date of mfr.: 1984–1988 *Approx. no. built:* 143

Early B39-8: Long with squared-off radiators and dynamic-brake housings. Longer, squarer nose (beveled twice) than the Dash-7 series. Break in the hood remains but air intakes around radiator air intake appear scattered. Box behind cab is higher than cab. Floating-bolster trucks. Surprisingly small windshield. Battery box step up to cab is on right side only. Thicker frame profile with access panels under cab is on left side only.

Later B39-8: Has canted radiator air intakes, more rational layout of small air intakes, and rearranged openings at dynamic-brake box. Box now lines up with cab roof. There is no break in hood aft of engine access doors.

The Dash-8 series brings us to the design style we see today from GE; massive machines with angular bumps and boxes all over, especially the winglike radiators. The boxy housings reflect what's inside as the computerized energy control system employs separate blowers for radiator fans, dynamic brakes, and traction motors in order to operate them only when needed. Previous systems used engine-driven central blowers and fans for cooling equipment and radiators, a continual drain on horsepower. This microcomputer system is the main technical feature of the Dash-8 series that distinguishes it from its predecessors.

GE B40-8

Length: 66 ft. 4 in. *Horsepower:* 4,000 *Cyl.:* 16
Date of mfr.: 1988-present *Approx. no. built:* 150

This current basic model is similar to the B39-8 but is offered in various forms including the wide cab B40-8W (see page 77) and the Amtrak Genesis (see page 97).

GE B32-8

Length: 63 ft. 7 in. *Horsepower:* 3,150 *Cyl.:* 12
Date of mfr.: 1984–1989 *Approx. no. built:* 49

A shorter version of the early B39-8, using the 12-cylinder engine, thus having only six tall access doors per side. The six doors are diagnostic when seen with the radiator wings and dynamic-brake hump. Retains the break in hood width ahead of radiators. Floating-bolster trucks. A special B32-8 has been built for Amtrak but differs in some important ways. See page 76 in the wide-cab section.

ROAD SWITCHERS/HIGH HOOD/B-B

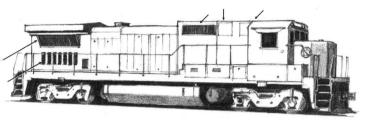

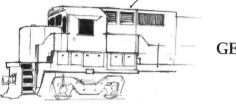

GE B39-8

GE B40-8

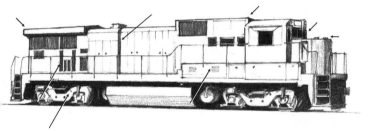

Early GE B39-8

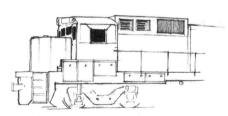

Alco RSD12, RSD15

Length: RSD12 58 ft. 1¾ in.; RSD15 66 ft. 7 in. *Horsepower:*
RSD12 1,800; RSD15 2,400 *Cyl.:* RSD12 12; RSD15 16
Date of mfr.: RSD12 1956–1963; RSD15 1956–1960
Approx. no. built: RSD12 161; RSD15 87

Alco's first six-axle road switchers, they appear as stretched
RS11s (see page 26). Distinctive Alco hood notches with C-C
trucks is diagnostic. The very rare RSD15 has an obviously
longer short hood and has seven square filters along each side of
the hood. The RSD12 has six. Note the Alco road trucks with
unevenly spaced axles.

The RSD15 was based on the earlier RSD7, now extinct. The
only RSD17 built, the Montreal Locomotive Works version of
the RSD7, still works for CP Rail. It lacks the notched hood but
is otherwise similar. A few dozen RSD12s remain in service.

EMD SD7, SD9, SD18

Length: 60 ft. 8½ in. *Horsepower:* SD7 1,500; SD9 1,750;
SD18 1,800 *Cyl.:* 16 *Date of mfr.:* SD7 1952–1953;
SD9 1954–1959; SD18 1960–1963 *Approx. no.
built:* SD7 188; SD9 471; SD18 54

A long diesel locomotive for its time, it has some interesting detail for train spotters. Radiator grilles project from hood sides.
Four small, round rooftop cooling fans are hidden behind a pipe
rail. When dynamic brakes are present, there are two additional
cooling fans over the blister. Frame profile shows a continuous
row of small, hinged access doors, sometimes louvered. Ladders
rather than grabirons were installed at the ends but may now
have been changed. The SD9 changed only the classification
lights, moving them out to the corners of the pointed, but
blunted hood. Any low-nosed SD7s or SD9s seen are home-
made. A few SD18s were originally built that way.

EMD developed a new six-axle road switcher rather than
basing it on their four-axle chassis as other manufacturers did,
hence its unique character. Although SD7s and SD18s are quite
rare, hundreds of SD9s are still at work.

EMD SD24

Length: 60 ft. 8½ in. *Horsepower:* 2,400 *Cyl.:* 16
Date of mfr.: 1958–1963 *Approx. no. built:* 179

Extremely rare, the turbocharged version of EMD's early six-
axle road switchers can be identified by the lowered roof section
(for air reservoirs) at the turbocharger stack. Also note the
rounded blower housing on the left side only and the screened
radiator shutters. Worth watching for.

ROAD SWITCHERS/HIGH HOOD/C-C

Alco RSD12

EMD SD7

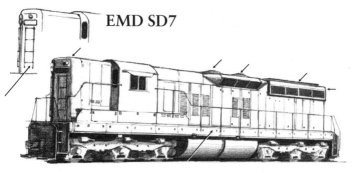

EMD SD9

Low-nosed
EMD SD18

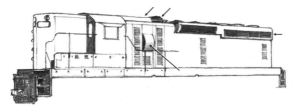

EMD SD24

EMD SD35, SDP35

Length: 60 ft. 8 in. *Horsepower:* 2,500 *Cyl.:* 16
Date of mfr.: 1964–1966 *Approx. no. built:* SD35 360;
SDP35 35

A short, typical EMD locomotive that looks to be all wheels on its six-axle trucks. The hood roof is all fans if equipped with dynamic braking; two for the dynamic brakes plus one small and two large radiator cooling fans. The fuel tank is noticeably short, to fit between the trucks. A single turbocharger stack shows just ahead of the dynamic brake cooling fans. There are ten handrail supports. The passenger version, the SDP35, had extra length at the rear of the hood to house a steam generator, and an extended walkway around the flat end of the hood. An extra bulge on the left behind the radiator area also identifies the SDP35, but it is feared they are no longer running.

The SD28 was an 1,800-horsepower version added to the line in 1965, but only six were sold. Two are thought to be still in service doing shortline work. They are identical to the SD35 except for having only two radiator cooling fans and two engine exhausts rather than the turbocharger stack.

EMD SD38, SD38-2

Length: SD38 65 ft. 9½ in.; SD38-2 68 ft. 10 in.
Horsepower: 2,000 *Cyl.:* 16 *Date of mfr.:* SD38 1967–1971;
SD38-2 1972–1979 *Approx. no. built:* SD38 53; SD38-2 81

Two radiator cooling fans and two exhaust stacks separate the SD38 and SD38-2 from the units that came before and after. Also note the projecting paper air-filter box behind the equipment air intake (not always present). This combination on six-axle trucks spells SD38 or SD38-2. As in the "General Purpose" or GP line, the Dash-2 can be identified by the oblong water-level sight glass on the right rear hood and the bolted rather than hinged battery boxes. However in the SD series there is another difference. The SD38-2 rides on a 3-ft.-longer platform giving it an especially stretched-out look with its long porches at either end.

Not big sellers by EMD standards, the SD38 and SD38-2 paved the way for the enormously successful SD40-2 (see page 56).

ROAD SWITCHERS/HIGH HOOD/C-C

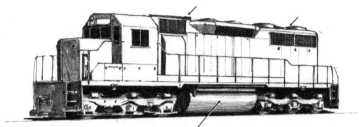

EMD SD35

EMD SDP35

EMD SD38-2, SD38

EMD SD39

Length: 65 ft. 9½ in. *Horsepower:* 2,300 *Cyl.:* 12
Date of mfr.: 1968–1970 *Approx. no. built:* 54

Another typical EMD diesel of the '70s. Looking like a GP38 on a longer platform, the SD39 is identified by the turbocharger stack just behind the air-filter housing. Or it could be called an SD38 with a tubocharged 12-cylinder engine. Two rooftop radiator cooling fans. Standard frame profile. Blower duct on the left side. Eleven handrail stanchions. As with the SD38, it was dropped with the arrival of the Dash-2 series. Thirty or so are in service and widely scattered.

EMD SDL39

Length: 55 ft. 2 in. *Horsepower:* 2,300 *Cyl.:* 12
Date of mfr.: 1969-1972 *Approx. no. built:* 10

Very short EMD-type locomotive. Seems to hardly have room for a fuel tank. Two cooling fans and no dynamic-brake housing. Standard EMD cab. Unique asymmetrical trucks. Nine handrail stanchions.

Included here because of their interest rather than the likelihood you will find one, except in the upper Midwest. The SDL39 is a novel version of the standard EMD look-alike, diesel road switchers. Unusual in the modern locomotive business, it was built specifically to bring big power to Milwaukee Road branch-line service in the early '70s. To save weight, the standard SD39 frame was shortened considerably and the lighter (and shorter) turbocharged 12-cylinder engine was used along with special trucks not seen elsewhere in North America. At this writing, all nine remaining SDL39s are in use on short hauls and branch-line service with Wisconsin Central.

ROAD SWITCHERS/HIGH HOOD/C-C

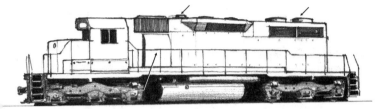

EMD SD39

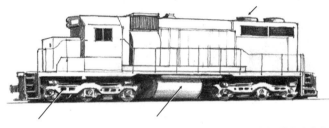

EMD SDL39

EMD SD40, SD40-2

Length: SD40 65 ft. 9½ in.; SD40-2 68 ft. 10 in.
Horsepower: 3,000 *Cyl.:* 16 *Date of mfr.:* SD40 1966–1972;
SD40-2 1972–1986 *Approx. no. built:* SD40 1,257;
SD40-2 3,947

Three radiator cooling fans, two dynamic-brake fans, and a turbocharger stack distinguish the SD40 series from the SD38. The SD45 series is similar but with slanted radiator air intakes. The Dash-2 here again, as in the SD38-2, is longer, and even though the hood is slightly longer, the 3 extra ft. of frame length increase the depth of the front and rear platforms noticeably from those of the SD40 (note that the last wheel on the rear truck is entirely out from under the hood). Except for Conrail's order, SD40-2s were equipped with EMD's high-traction truck (three holes in a row on the truck frame between wheels). An extended-nose model was built for Union Pacific, Kansas City Southern, and Southern Pacific. The low nose, known as the snoot, is about 3 ft. longer, using up most of the front porch, and houses radio control equipment.

EMD's great success story, the SD40 and SD40-2 are as common as house sparrows and seen on railroads large and small. Despite the presence of the more powerful SD45, the reliability and versatility of the 16-cylinder SD40-2 made it EMD's biggest seller of all time and the standard of the industry.

Several interesting variations were offered over the 22-year production period. Eighteen SD40As were built on the 70-ft.-8-in. SDP45 frame for Illinois Central, who still operate a dozen of them. They are recognizable by the extra hood length seen between the dynamic-brake blister and the radiator air intakes. Also note the extra-long fuel tank, the reason they were conceived. The SDP40 (six for Great Northern and fourteen for Mexican National) were passenger versions. The radiators are pushed forward with the dynamic-brake housing to make room for the steam generator compartment with its own air grille. Perhaps eight are still running south of the border.

CP Rail bought 25 SD40-2Fs with a full envelope body (see page 108), while Canadian National ordered theirs with the Canadian style Comfort Cab (see page 78). The tunnel version, a major variation, is illustrated on page 61.

ROAD SWITCHERS/HIGH HOOD/C-C

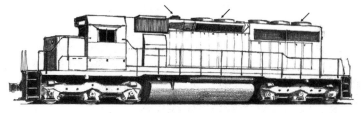

EMD SD40

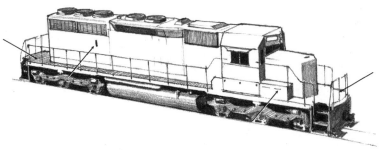

EMD SD40-2

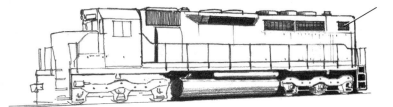

EMD SDP40

EMD SD45, SD45-2

Length: SD45 65 ft. 9½ in.; SD45-2 68 ft. 10 in.
Horsepower: 3,600 *Cyl.:* 20 *Date of mfr.:* SD45 1965–1971;
SD45-2 1972–1974 *Approx. no. built:* SD45 1,260; SD45-2
136

Until the just-announced SD80MAC, the SD45 was the only six-axle EMD unit with flared radiator air intakes. Dynamic-brake housing fairs neatly into the three screened radiator inlets, making a continuous bulge. Three radiator cooling fans. It is the same length as an SD40, but the longer hood fills in the porches. The SD45-2 reverts to flat radiator intakes. As with the SD38 and SD39 series, the Dash-2 model is 3 ft. longer and rides on high-traction trucks. Lengthening the radiators flattened the air inlets and spread the rooftop cooling fans noticeably farther apart.

Determined to win the horsepower race, EMD went to a 20-cylinder version of their standard engine, and although it sold well initially, interest was fading by the time the Dash-2 modifications appeared. Maintaining the bigger fuel-guzzling engine and its accompanying gear was not necessarily worth 600 extra horsepower, and although many of the locomotive's problems were solved in the SD45-2 model, it was the SD40-2 that went on to become EMD's star in the '80s. As they fell from favor with the big railroads, the '45s' low price made them attractive to a variety of smaller operations, and they can now be seen in such unlikely places as New Mexico's Southwestern Railroad (one SD45) and Guilford's Springfield (Mass.) Terminal (five SD45s). Montana Rail Link and Wisconsin Central operate fleets of both the SD45 and SD45-2.

A variant is the extremely rare SDP45, stretched to 70 ft. 8 in. to provide space for a steam generator. This strategy was similar to that behind the SD40A (see page 56) and only a little more successful, with most being sold for freight use. The 4,200-horsepower SD40X is notable as the test bed for Dash-2 modifications, including the high-traction truck. Only seven were built, and none remain, a high-horsepower idea whose time had not yet come.

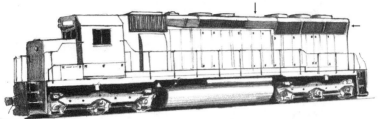

EMD SD45

EMD SDP45

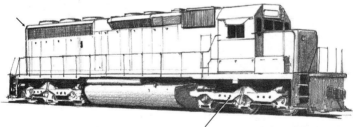

EMD SD45-2

EMD SD40T-2, SD45T-2

Length: 70 ft. 8 in. *Horsepower:* SD40T-2 3,000;
SD45T-2 3,600 *Cyl.:* SD40T-2 16; SD45T-2 20
Date of mfr.: SD40T-2 1974–1980; SD45T-2 1972–1975
Approx. no. built: SD40T-2 310; SD45T-2 247

Very long hood with top-mounted radiators and low air intakes just above walkway. These features combined with EMD cab and high-traction trucks are diagnostic for the *tunnel motors* as they are often called. Also note typical EMD dynamic brake housing, equipment blower duct, and curved fuel tank. Although quite different mechanically, the two locomotives appear similar from the outside. However, the SD45T-2 has a longer hood pushing the cab forward and using up the front platform space, unlike the SD40T-2. This is expressed in the wider space between the dynamic-brake-grid air inlet and the radiators. A detail difference that is useful close-up is the number of cooling fan access doors under the radiators. The SD40T-2 has two, the SD45T-2, three. Some of Southern Pacific's first orders of the SD40T-2 included a 3-ft.-longer nose (the snoot) to house radio control equipment, giving the units a definite character of their own. Sources differ as to the overall length of these locomotives, but the EMD drawings are quite clear. All tunnel models including the snoot are 70 ft. 8 in. from inside one coupler face to the other.

Railroad fans are drawn to special adaptations in locomotive design, and the solution EMD came up with to improve cooling in tunnels is a favorite. After trying several devices to avoid overheating in tunnels on routes through the Rockies and Sierra Nevadas, the designers decided to mount the radiators high in the hood with fans on the cool side drawing air in low and blowing it up through the radiators and out the top. The idea was to use the cooler air found lower in the tunnel, and judging from the sales to mountain railroads, the idea must have worked pretty well. (Others have pointed out that the modification greatly resembles Alco engineering practice as illustrated in their Century series locomotives of ten years earlier. See pages 26–27).

Southern Pacific and the Denver and Rio Grande were the only customers, and now, with the Rio Grande's absorption by SP, the tunnel motors are under one flag. They roam far, however, and can be spotted all across the country.

ROAD SWITCHERS/HIGH HOOD/C-C

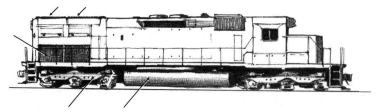

EMD SD40T-2

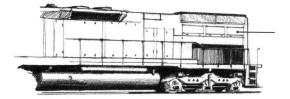

EMD SD45T-2

Alco C-628, C-630, C-636

Length: 69 ft. *Horsepower:* C-628 2,750; C-630 3,000; C-636 3,600 *Cyl.:* 16 *Date of mfr.:* C-628 1963–1968; C-630 1965–1969; C-636 1967–1968 *Approx. no. built:* C-628 181; C-630 133; C-636 34

The C-628 is a long locomotive with a very clean roofline and a curious radiator arrangement. Good field marks are the typical Alco notched long hood (a few were built with a notched high short hood and were intended to run long hood forward). The round-roofed cab is well forward, leaving a stubby nose but accentuating the unit's length. Cab front is pointed with a two-piece windshield. Large cylindrical fuel tanks. Air reservoirs on right side only. A small rectangular air intake is located almost midway down the hood on each side and is sometimes hooded. The C-628 runs on the Alco road trucks with unequally spaced axles.

The C-630 is similar but with a prominent aftercooler box assembly. The C-636 has an additional rooftop box just ahead of the radiators.

The Century series, both four- and six-axle, was designed to compete with EMD's GP30 and GE's U25B, but the numbers indicate Alco's dwindling fortunes in the 1960s. Dozens of C-630s are still around, here and in Mexico, as well as a few C-628s, but the C-636s are all but gone.

The last Alco C-630s were built in Canada, followed by the Montreal Locomotive Work's own versions, the M630 and M636. There were few differences as the sketch shows. The aftercooler box was smaller and framed differently, and the radiator housing of the M630 had a bevel to the forward edge. BC Rail at one time had several M630Ws with the Canadian Comfort Cab (see M424W entry). A number of the MLW locomotives are still operating in Canada and Mexico. (A single M640 was built and is listed with Canadian National Railways. If you spot an M636 with a GE-type winged radiator assembly, you've found it.)

ROAD SWITCHERS/HIGH HOOD/C-C

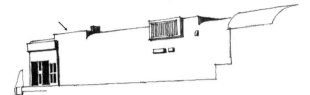

Alco C-636

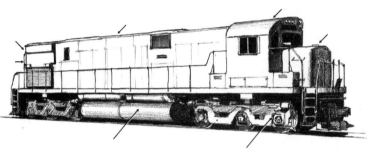

Alco C-628

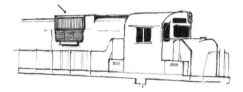

Alco C-630

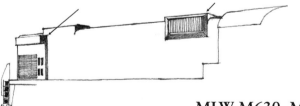

MLW M630, M636

GE U25C, U28C

Length: 67 ft. 3 in. *Horsepower:* U25C 2,500; U28C 2,800
Cyl.: 16 *Date of mfr.:* U25C 1963–1965; U28C 1965–1966
Approx. no. built: U25C 113; U28C 71

GE's first six-axle road switchers, the U25C and U28C are all but gone. Recognizable by the simple radiator screen, the step up in the walkway at the radiator end of the platform, and the double-equalized trucks, the U25C and early U28C were virtually identical. Late U28Cs more closely resemble U30Cs but lack the widening of the hood at the radiators. They rode on an early version of the floating-bolster truck.

GE U23C

Length: 67 ft. 3 in. *Horsepower:* 2,250–2,300 *Cyl.:* 12
Date of mfr.: 1968–1970 *Approx. no. built:* 53

Not to miss out in the intermediate-horsepower market, GE put a 12-cylinder engine on a U30C platform. To find one of the score that remain, you will have to count tall engine access door panels. The U23C has only six on each side.

GE U30C

Length: 67 ft. 3 in. *Horsepower:* 3,000 *Cyl.:* 16
Date of mfr.: 1967–1976 *Approx. no. built:* 600

Simple, clean long hood with cab well forward and very short nose. Flat face with two-piece windshield. Extra side windows. Hood is wider at the radiator area. Typical GE angular fuel tank. Long raised step at rear of cab on both sides. The eight tall access door panels on each side indicate a 16-cylinder engine. GE floating-bolster trucks. Note the minor differences at the radiator area on early U30Cs.

The best seller by far of the six-axle "U-boats" was the U30C, developed from GE's experiences with the less popular U28C and U25C. More than a hundred are still pulling trains here and in Mexico.

GE U33C, U36C

Length: 67 ft. 3 in. *Horsepower:* U33C 3,300; U36C 3,600
Cyl.: 16 *Date of mfr.:* U33C 1968–1975; U36C 1971–1975
Approx. no. built: U33C 375; U36C 218

Very similar to the U30C, these indistinguishable locomotives represented evolutionary horsepower increases. Good field marks for both are the beginnings of the winged radiator assemblies found on all subsequent GE road diesels. U33Cs have nearly vanished but a hundred or so U36Cs remain in service.

ROAD SWITCHERS/HIGH HOOD/C-C

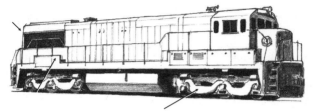

GE U25C, Early U28C

GE U23C, Early U30C

Late GE U28C

GE U33C, U36C

GE U30C

GE/AT&SF SF30C

Length: 67 ft. 3 in. *Horsepower:* 3,100 *Cyl.:* 16
Date of mfr.: 1985–1987 *Approx. no. built:* 70

The Santa Fe shops rebuilt U36Cs adding more sophisticated electronics and making them easier to maintain. Visually, the differences are subtle. Look for a "U-boat" with a later-model, less-rounded GE nose. The break in the hood comes well forward of the radiator intakes on the right, while on the left there is a bulge housing the tilted oil cooler. All are in Santa Fe paint at this writing. The step up to the rear of the cab is much shorter on the left, and the frame profile is straight. Other details are generally similar to those of the U36C.

GE C30-7, C36-7

Length: 67 ft. 3 in. *Horsepower:* C30-7 3,000; C36-7 3,600
Cyl.: 16 *Date of mfr.:* C30-7 1976–1985; C36-7 1978–1985
Approx. no. built: C30-7 1,137; C36-7 169

Long, clean "U-boat"-looking locomotives. Snub-nosed with radiator wings. The break in hood width has moved forward, the identifying feature of Dash-7 units. Also note the air intakes arranged around the radiator grille. Cabs usually lack the extra side windows, but early models may show blank panels. Late C36-7s have dynamic-brake grids in a high box behind the cab. Different large air intakes are below the box on either side.

This very successful line helped put GE ahead of the field in locomotive sales. More than a thousand C30-7s still roam the continent, with more than a hundred C36-7s representing almost all their production. After 1983 the C36-7s were equipped with what became Dash-8 features, visibly the dynamic brakes described above. These locomotives were rated at 3,750 horsepower. However, Conrail ordered 25 of the later models without the dynamic brakes just to confuse spotters. But they can be identified by the late-model air-intake arrangement at the rear.

GE C30-7A

Length: 67 ft. 3 in. *Horsepower:* 3,000 *Cyl.:* 12
Date of mfr.: 1984 *Approx. no. built:* 50

The 12-cylinder engine that had been so successful in the B30-7A four-axle locomotive was combined with the six-axle Dash-7 series in the C30-7A. Conrail was the only customer before the model was replaced with the C32-8 just months later (see page 68). Both have the six tall engine access doors associated with the 12-cylinder engine. The C30-7A is otherwise similar to the late C36-7.

ROAD SWITCHERS/HIGH HOOD/C-C

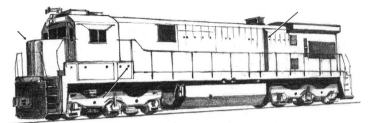

GE/AT&SF SF30C

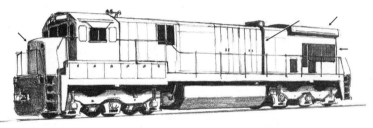

GE C30-7, Early C36-7

GE C30-7A

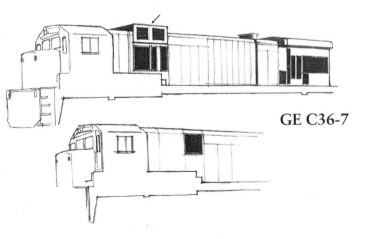

GE C36-7

GE C39-8, C39-8E

Length: 70 ft. 8 in. *Horsepower:* 3,900 *Cyl.:* 16
Date of mfr.: 1983–1987 *Approx. no. built:* 162

Huge hump behind the cab, wide radiators, and hard-edged cab/nose styling of the C39-8 established GE's current design character. Hood openings in hump differ on right and left sides. The break in hood width ahead of the radiators is continued. The many small air intakes below the radiators seem scattered. There are eight full-height engine access doors. Angular fuel tanks.

The enhanced C39-8E is a forerunner of the Dash-9 series, with its angled radiator grilles and organized small air intakes. The cab is raised and flattened to line up with the hood and there is a step up to the cab on the left as well as the right side. The break in the hood is gone. The radiators are bulkier. Only 25 were built, all for Norfolk Southern Railway.

The Dash-8 series is visually distinct from earlier GE locomotives (and any others for that matter) but is very similar to the later Dash-9 and AC44CW models. The success of the Dash-8 line and its computer-controlled management of auxiliary systems and wheel slip enabled GE to outsell its rival, EMD, for the first time, and GE has held the lead since.

GE C32-8

Length: 67 ft. 11 in. *Horsepower:* 3,150 *Cyl.:* 12
Date of mfr.: 1984–present *Approx. no. built:* 10

GE keeps its 12-cylinder prime mover in the catalog with the C32-8. Similar to the C39-8, it can be identified by the six tall access doors on each side. Although nearly 3 ft. shorter than the C39-8, the length difference is not obvious. All ten were originally built for Conrail.

ROAD SWITCHERS/HIGH HOOD/C-C

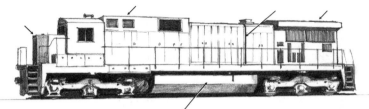

GE C39-8

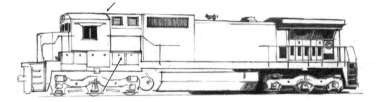

GE C39-8E

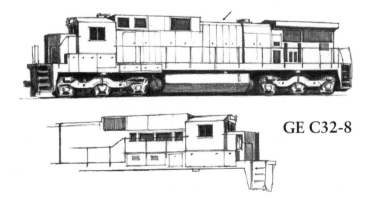

GE C32-8

GE C40-8

Length: 70 ft. 8 in. *Horsepower:* 4,000 *Cyl.:* 16
Date of mfr.: 1987–present *Approx. no. built:* 655

Wide wings with canted radiator grilles and small intakes neatly lined up beneath. The cab appears to have been raised and flattened to match the hood and the break in the hood is gone. A new brow over the windshield has the two headlights side-by-side rather than over-and-under. Nearly identical to the enhanced C39-8E, the C40-8 has the right-side fuel tank notched for the two air reservoirs.

The C40-8 is sold in two other versions: the full-bodied C40-8M Draper design and the wide-nosed C40-8W (see entries under full-width hood Draper and wide-nose sections).

If the Dash-7 series allowed GE to gain market share, then the Dash-8 line established GE's supremacy in diesel locomotive sales. Seen everywhere (though more often with the wide cab), Dash-8 diesels are symbolic of modern railroading. Confusion still abounds when it comes to GE's terminology. Should you come across reference to a Dash-840C, rest assured it is a C40-8. After several years of spelling out *Dash* the experiment has apparently ended and most writers have reverted to the original nomenclature of the mid-'80s.

A factory rebuild of older C30 locomotives, known as Super 7s, closely resembles C40-8s at first glance. However, the hump behind the cab and the cab itself are lower, and the air conditioning box sits outside on the cab roof. The headlight and number-board housing is smaller as well. Most have gone to Mexico, but Chicago and Northwestern, and Monongahela are reported to have bought a few.

GE C40-9

Length: 73 ft. 2 in. *Horsepower:* 4,000 *Cyl.:* 16
Date of mfr.: 1994–present

The only big, long GE Standard Cab locomotive riding on GE's new high-traction trucks is a C40-9, especially when in Norfolk Southern black. Very sharp cornered and angular, even to the air conditioning box atop the cab. It has the usual Dash-9 clues: shorter central air intake, three-beveled fuel tank (notched on the right for the air reservoirs), and the Dash-9 arrangement of air intakes under the radiators. Note the recessed brake wheel on the left.

The only Dash-9s built to date, they come loaded with all the accessories: electronics, computers, and recorders, but no wide-nosed cab. The last major railroad to order only Standard Cabs, Norfolk Southern was also the last to specify long-hood-forward operation, just a few years ago. Interestingly, their new C40-9s are delivered with ditch lights and full headlighting on both ends. They are not giving up.

ROAD SWITCHERS/HIGH HOOD/C-C

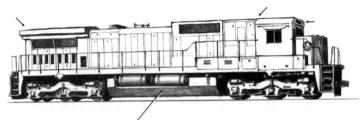

GE C40-8

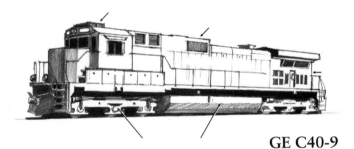

GE C40-9

EMD SD50, SD60

Length: 71 ft. 2 in. *Horsepower:* SD50 3,500–3,600; SD60 3,800 *Cyl.:* 16 *Date of mfr.:* SD50 1981–1985; SD60 1984–1991 *Approx. no. built:* SD50 421; SD60 601

Massive, clean-lined locomotives with the dynamic-brake intakes just ahead and below the central air intake and with a large dynamic-brake fan on top. Three radiator cooling fans. Pronounced overhang at front platform. Straight frame profile. Note the little hop in the left handrail to clear the blower duct.

To distinguish between the SD50 and SD60, you will have to count latched doors and door panels under the radiator inlet grilles. The SD50 reportedly has four latched panels out of six, while the SD60 sports six out of eight. Trucks are the high-traction type, although Conrail bought some SD50s with Flexicoil-type trucks.

The SD50/60 are noted for their microprocessor control systems, which necessitated some rearranging inside to accommodate electrical modules. This resulted in a new location for the dynamic-brake grids directly behind the cab, now a standard EMD field mark. SD50Fs were built for Canadian National using the Canadian Comfort Cab and Draper bodywork (see page 108). The SD60M was also offered in two American wide-nosed cab styles (see page 78).

EMD SD70

Length: 72 ft. 4 in. *Horsepower:* 4,000 *Cyl.:* 16 *Date of mfr.:* 1993–present

Longer still than the SD60, the SD70 has grown bumps and boxes although nothing like its GE counterparts. Just behind the cab on the left is a lengthened and louvered walkway box and a new-style blower duct. There is no horizontal duct along the walkway. On top, the exhaust silencer sits on a square box that projects well above the hood. The radiator section has been raised as well, interrupting the once smooth EMD roofline. An important field mark for spotters are the new radial trucks.

Direct competition with GE's very successful six-axle line, the SD70 relies on the new HTCR truck (high-traction, six-axle, radial) and much faster control-system computing as selling points, as well as more horsepower. The truck can steer through curves, thus reducing maintenance on both wheels and rails. The SD70 may be the last of the EMD Standard Cabs. Only the Norfolk Southern and Illinois Central have ordered the Standard Cab version of the SD70, but their units should be highly visible to railfans. Larger orders are for the SD70M and SD70MAC wide-nosed models (see page 80).

ROAD SWITCHERS/HIGH HOOD/C-C

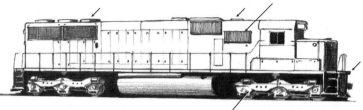

EMD SD50

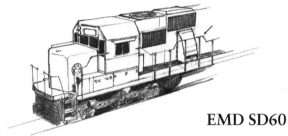

EMD SD60

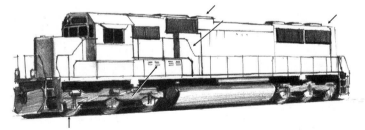

EMD SD70

MLW M420(W), M420R

Length: 60 ft. 10 in. *Horsepower:* 2,000 *Cyl.:* 12
Date of mfr.: 1973–1977 *Approx. no. built:* 97

Wide four-piece windshield in full-width cab made of flat planes and sharp, angular corners. Long hood is very clean with a typical Alco radiator detail at the rear. Angular fuel tank varies in length. Both air reservoirs are on the right side. Unusual MLW trucks. Not all units had dynamic braking and thus may lack the extra openings behind the central air intake. Note the pylon for mounting the bell and horns.

The first wide-nosed Comfort Cab anticipated the revolution in cab design that is going on more than 20 years later. Most of the Montreal Locomotive Work's production run is still at work for Canadian National Railways. Curiously, in the only sale of Canadian locomotives to the U.S., five M420s, called M420Rs, were built for the Providence and Worcester Railroad. They differed only in that they kept their Alco AAR-type trade-in trucks. The surviving three M420Rs now work on the Iowa Interstate Railroad.

The wide cab was also tried on ten M630Ws, the six-axle stretch model. One or two may still be running, according to some sources. A 2,400-horsepower version was sold to Mexican National Railways as the M424W, and most of the 72 ordered are still in service. The radiator detail is similar to the Alco Century-430 (see page 40). Finally, and much later in the early '80s, a very few HR412s, variant of the M420, were built by Bombardier, Inc., MLW's successor. Visually, it differs in the radiator area.

EMD GP38-2W, GP40-2W

Length: 59 ft. 2 in. *Horsepower:* GP38-2W 2,000; GP40-2W 3,000 *Cyl.:* 16 *Date of mfr.:* 1973–1974; GP40-2W 1972–1986 *Number built:* GP38-2W 51; GP40-2W 275

Built for Canadian National Railways, EMD's version of the Canadian Comfort Cab lines up the top of the four-piece windshield and softens the corners a bit. Compare with MLW M420(W) above. Equipment blower and electrical box on the left walkway behind the cab have been modified from the standard GP38-2 (see page 34). GP38-2Ws and GP40-2Ws did not come with dynamic braking. Otherwise note the typical GP38-2 details: two closely spaced cooling fans, two exhaust stacks, and the high air-filter box interrupting an otherwise sleek hood. The GP40-2W has the standard GP40-2 triple exhaust fan assembly and a smoother roof line without the air-filter box.

ROAD SWITCHERS/WIDE NOSE/B-B

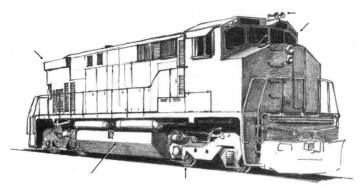

MLW M420

HR412   M424W

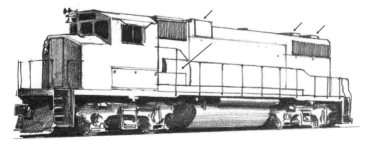

EMD GP38-2W

EMD GP60M

Length: 59 ft. 9 in. *Horsepower:* 3,800 *Cyl.:* 16
Date of mfr.: 1990 *Number built:* 61

EMD's two-piece windshield, North American wide cab. Pointed nose with door on the engineer's right pushing the headlights off-center. Angled glass in pointed windshield with only number boards above. Extra side window. Otherwise the GP60M resembles the standard GP60, with three cooling fans and equipment air intake behind cab. Frame profile is thin and straight. Blomberg trucks.

A handsome special-order locomotive for Santa Fe, always seen in their red, yellow, and silver warbonnet paint scheme. Look for them between Chicago and Los Angeles hauling long, intermodal freight trains at steady, high speeds, usually with matching B units.

GE B40-8W

Length: 66 ft. 4 in. *Horsepower:* 4,000 *Cyl.:* 16
Date of mfr.: 1990–present *Number built:* 83

GE's wide-nosed cab design drops the front corners for crew visibility and uses rectangular windshield glass. Windshield is raked but the number boards are vertical. Headlights are centered high on the nose. Nose access door is on the left of center (to the engineer) with a small window. Frame profile shows a dropped skirt under the cab and battery boxes on the right side similar to the left. Otherwise the B40-8W is the conventional cab B40-8 (see page 48) with angled radiator intakes, wide radiators, and a large hump behind the cab. Eight tall access doors per side indicate 16-cylinder power.

Sometimes referred to as Dash-840BWs these hefty units are, so far at least, found only on the Santa Fe in warbonnet paint.

GE B32-8WH(P32-8BWH)

Length: 66 ft. 4 in. *Horsepower:* 3,200 *Cyl.:* 12
Date of mfr.: 1991 *Number built:* 20

Seen only in Amtrak colors (with special striped paint job, at least initially), this locomotive is similar to the B40-8W, and most spotting marks apply. However, the six tall engine access doors betray the 12-cylinder prime mover inside.

This locomotive suffers from a classic terminology crisis in that Amtrak has given it their own designation, referring to it as a P32-8BWH (passenger, horsepower, Dash-8 series, four-axle, wide-nose, head-end power!). They are commonly called "P32s" and even "tugboats." GE generally agrees — but not in that order — and likes to include "W" for wide cab, ignoring the "P." Still others use past GE practice of putting *Dash* first as in Dash8-32BWH. Whatever.

ROAD SWITCHERS/WIDE NOSE/B-B

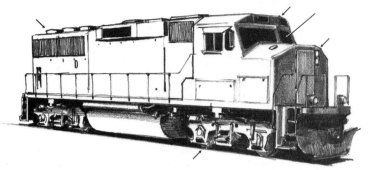

EMD GP60M

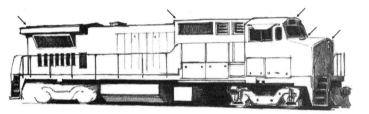

GE B40-8W

EMD SD40-2(W)

Length: 68 ft. 10 in. *Horsepower:* 3,000 *Cyl.:* 16
Date of mfr.: 1975–1980 *Approx. no. built:* 123

Canadian National's Comfort Cab variant of the well-known SD40-2, with four-piece windshield, is identified by the EMD-style hood and frame on six-axle trucks and the deep platforms front and rear. Watch for other typical SD40-2 field marks: three cooling fans (plus two dynamic-brake cooling fans), two exhaust stacks, notched frame profile at air reservoirs, water-level sight gauge, and equipment blower duct on the left.

All other EMD Canadian Comfort Cab units, except the GP38-2W, were full-width hood Draper types. Nearly all of the SD40-2(W)s are currently in operation with Canadian National Railways, the only buyer.

EMD SD60M, SD60I

Length: 71 ft. 2 in. *Horsepower:* 3,800 *Cyl.:* 16
Date of mfr.: 1989–present *Number built:* 500+

Three radiator cooling fans. Dynamic-brake gear moved to just behind the cab with air intake ahead of and below central intake. New-type blower duct with bump in handrail. There is no step in the walkway up to the cab on the left side. Simple, thin frame profile. Standard EMD road trucks.

The wide cab is seen in three versions. Illustrated is the vertical, three-piece type with a small, flat center section and the adjacent glass slightly swept back. There is a small brow over the center window. The slightly pointed nose is flat on top with beveled edges matching the eaves of the cab roof. The headlights are centered high and number boards to either side. An access door without a window is left of the centerline. Soo Line, Burlington Northern, and Union Pacific bought this model.

The second cab design has the two-piece, raked and pointed windshield seen on the GP60M (page 77). The top front of the cab is bent vertical with side-by-side headlights and number boards. The nose is pointed and the access door is to the left with a small window. The top of the hood is flat with beveled edges, and the latest models have a second bevel allowing the crew to see the front steps. Conrail and Union Pacific are users.

The third version is similar to the second but the cab is isolated from the rest of the locomotive with thick gasketing. An isolating seam can be seen around the nose. The access door, with window, is on the right. This acoustic and vibration isolation is apparently important since a separate designation, SD60I, has been granted. Conrail ordered 90 units, half to be assembled from kits at Conrail's own shops in Altoona, Pa. Growing more common by the week, the SD60M has been ordered in quantity by at least four major U.S. railroads.

ROAD SWITCHERS/WIDE NOSE/C-C

EMD SD40-2(W)

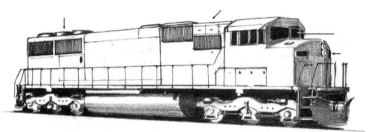

EMD SD60M

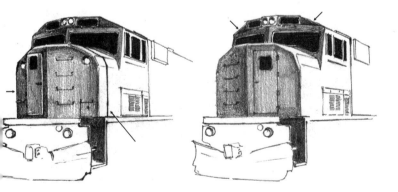

EMD SD60I   EMD SD60M

EMD SD70M, SD75M

Length: 72 ft. 4 in. (73 ft. 2 in.) *Horsepower:* SD70M 4,000; SD75M 4,300–4,500 *Cyl.:* 16 *Date of mfr.:* 1992–present *Approx. no. built:* 121

A very long locomotive on EMD's new HTC high-traction, six-axle trucks. Note the additional hood opening under the radiator air inlets on the left side and a recessed brake wheel near the same spot on the right. There is also a long step up to the cab on the left and a very short step on the right. The blower duct under the central air intake on the left is a simple box shape. Three radiator cooling fans at the rear and one dynamic-brake fan up front, just behind the cab. Only the two-piece windshield cab is used on SD70Ms with the door on the right front unlike the early demonstrators.

Southern Pacific, Canadian National, and Santa Fe have ordered this locomotive. Santa Fe calls theirs SD75M for the increased horsepower. They appear to have a blower duct on each side but are otherwise identical to the SD70M.

EMD SD70MAC

Length: 74 ft. *Horsepower:* 4,000 *Cyl.:* 16 *Date of mfr.:* 1993–present

Very similar visually to the SD70M, the "Big Mac" can be told from the others by the additional air inlets under the dynamic-brake air inlet and under the radiator air intakes on each side of the hood for cooling the inverters. Also, the right side blower duct is the type used on the SD50 and SD60. The extra length of the SD70MAC is noticeable where the hood extends past the radiator grilles at the rear. The cab is EMD's later two-piece-windshield type with the nose door on the left.

Burlington Northern was the first customer for this new breed of locomotive from EMD, ordering 380 units to upgrade their coal-hauling operation out of Montana and Wyoming. Unit reduction is BN's goal, and three SD70MACs are replacing five older units on most coal trains. The SD70MACs are EMD's attempt to assert themselves once again as leaders in the diesel locomotive market, having lost the lead to GE in the 1980s. The alternating current (AC) power system combined with the new radial truck has reportedly resulted in reduced wear and maintenance costs. Electrical equipment including alternators and AC traction motors are from Siemens Transportation Systems.

The four three-piece windshield versions are actually earlier 3,800-horsepower SD60MACs, built in 1991 to test the radial truck and AC traction systems.

More powerful 80-ft., 2-in. SD80 and 90MACs have been ordered by Conrail and Union Pacific. All are available with the isolated cab. See the SD60I on page 79. Note the canted radiator assembly.

ROAD SWITCHERS/WIDE NOSE/C-C

EMD SD70M

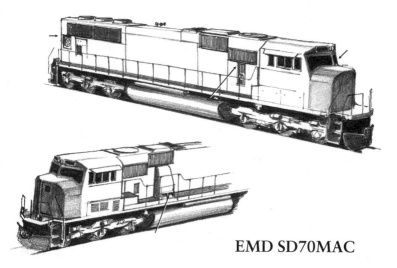

EMD SD70MAC

EMD SD80/90MAC

GE C40-8W, C41-8W

Length: 70 ft. 8 in. *Horsepower:* 4,000 (C41-8W, 4,135)
Cyl.: 16 *Date of mfr.:* 1989 (C41-8W, 1993)
Approx no. built: 875 (C41-8W, 163)

GE's wide-nosed cab on a C40-8 (or a Dash-8-40C if you prefer). Angular, sharp-edged appearance. Two-piece windshield is pointed and raked, but glass is nearly rectangular (compare to SD70M). GE drops the corners of the nose (so the crew can see who is standing on the steps), giving the C40-8W a high-cheekboned look. Nose door with a small window is on the left of center. Other details are typical for all C40-8 series: angular fuel tanks notched on the right side for air reservoirs, huge radiators spread across the top rear of the hood (supported by flared air intakes), and a long hump behind the cab.

Kicking off what some observers call the third generation of the diesel era, the Dash-8 established GE as the number one U.S. locomotive builder. The C40-8W is the culmination of that series and continues the microprocessor-controlled, high-horsepower evolution with a modern cab design. A slightly more powerful model, the C41-8W has been purchased in quantity by Union Pacific, but no reliable spotting feature is known. Fifty 4,400-horsepower units were built for CSX and should properly be called C44-8Ws, but CSX lists them as C44-9Ws for no known reason. See the next entry for the real C44-9W.

GE C44-9W

Length: 73 ft. 2 in. *Horsepower:* 4,400 *Cyl.:* 16
Date of mfr.: 1993–present

A still longer version of the six-axle GE front-runner. Important field mark is the new high-adhesion truck, a unique design. More gently beveled fuel tank but still notched on the right side for air reservoirs. Radiators are thicker although that detail began in late Dash-8 production. The central air intake is considerably shorter than on the Dash-8 series. There are a few more small air intakes under the radiators. The aft air intakes have been rearranged on the left, and a ninth one has been added on the right. The brake wheel is centered under the radiators on the left side and four square intakes appear just forward of it.

The first wide-nosed locomotive purchase by Southern Pacific leaves only archconservative Norfolk Southern holding out for Standard Cabs. (NS has recently obtained 125 4,000-horsepower versions of this locomotive with the Standard Cab. See page 70.)

ROAD SWITCHERS/WIDE NOSE/C-C

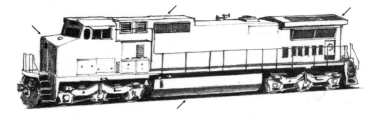

GE C40-8W, C41-8W

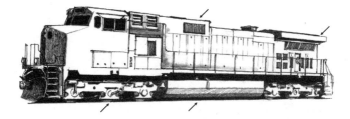

GE C44-9W

GE AC4400CW

Length: 73 ft. 2 in. *Horsepower:* 4,400 *Cyl.:* 16
Date of mfr.: 1994–present

Typical long, bumpy GE roofline. Similar to C44-9W but with large AC equipment box on left side behind cab. Central air intake is now small, but additional dynamic-brake cooling grids have been added to the hump. Look for the new air conditioning location under the cab windows on the right side. Also, air inlets under the right side radiators have been lined up. High-traction bolsterless trucks.

GE's state-of-the-art locomotive is selling well. CSX, Chicago and North Western, Canadian Pacific, and Union Pacific are customers. Union Pacific and CSX are also down for the forthcoming 3-ft.-longer 6,000-horsepower model, the AC6000CW.

Morrison Knudsen MK5000C

Length: 73 ft. 4 in. *Horsepower:* 5,000 *Cyl.:* 12
Date of mfr.: 1994–present

A big brute of a locomotive with its blunt, bulldog nose accentuated by the sharply sloped corners. Very clean hood and roofline with four radiator cooling fans. Hood air inlets are in the usual places. Unique high-adhesion trucks appear on no other U.S. locomotive. Cab looks like a cross between GE's and EMD's latest: the angular windows of an SD70M with sloped nose of a C44-9W, but the access door is on the centerline (with small window). Note the graceful EMD-type fuel tank.

The first new Class 1 locomotive builder in decades, MK Rail jumped into the new diesel-locomotive business with the most powerful units to date. However, MK is no stranger to the railroad industry, having had many successes in the areas of commuter rail equipment and major locomotive remanufacturing programs. Interesting features of the MK5000C are the Caterpillar prime mover and MK's own six-axle trucks. Southern Pacific is trying out three units and Union Pacific is to follow with three more. It is hoped that the financial difficulties of parent company Morrison Knudsen Corporation will not hinder the development of the MK5000C. An AC version is reportedly in the works.

GE AC4400CW

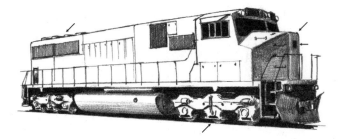

MK5000C

EMD DD40AX Centennial

Length: 98 ft. 5 in. *Horsepower:* 2 × 3,300 *Cyl.:* 2 × 16
Date of mfr.: 1969–1971 *Number built:* 47

Unmistakable. Looking like an A and B unit welded together, the Centennial is nearly 100 ft. long with huge four-axle trucks and enormous fuel tanks. Six radiator cooling fans and two dynamic-brake fans are spread along the hood on a continuous, flared housing that rises to create a long hump containing both sets of radiator shutters and dynamic-brake air inlets. A transverse tunnel amidships allows additional access from side to side. Typical EMD details are evident, such as the blower duct and filtered central air intakes.

The DD40AX is in effect a double GP40. Intended to accomplish unit reduction by combining two locomotives in one, the unit also functioned as a test bed for the modular electrical components that would become the Dash-2 improvements in EMD's line of road switchers. The name *Centennial* was to honor the 100th anniversary of the Golden Spike ceremony and the country's first transcontinental railroad.

Built only for Union Pacific, the DD40AX is important enough to include here, despite there being only two left in operation; one with Union Pacific and the other with Dakota Southern. Both are in active service and not museum pieces, but you will have to head west to see them in action.

ROAD SWITCHERS/WIDE NOSE

EMD DD40AX

EMD F40C

Length: 68 ft. 10 in. *Horsepower:* 3,200 *Cyl.:* 16
Date of mfr.: 1974 *Number built:* 15

A shortened SDP40F, the F40C is recognized by its corrugated side panels and its location; all 15 pull commuter trains in the Chicago area. Note the similarities to the SDP40F: high-traction trucks, no nose platform, and identical side-panel arrangement. Note the blunt nose.

With an alternator instead of steam generators for passenger train requirements, the F40C could be shorter. But its otherwise similarity to the ill-fated SDP40F spelled sales trouble and, except for Metra, the Chicago area commuter service, it was passed over by commuter railroads for the F40PH.

EMD SDP40F

Length: 72 ft. 4 in. *Horsepower:* 3,000 *Cyl.:* 16
Date of mfr.: 1973–1974 *Number built:* 150

At first the SDP40F looks like an FP45 on high-traction trucks, but there are clear visual differences. Most importantly, the radiators were moved forward (note the shorter 16-cylinder engine) making room for a noticeably larger and quite different steam generator area. The cab was also moved forward slightly, but this is not as obvious after front platforms were added by Santa Fe shops. Minor differences in air intake sizes and shapes exist, but the lack of a porthole in a single access door is a better field mark. Earliest units had a pointed nose; later ones were flat. Otherwise typical details abound: three cooling fans, beveled hood with air inlets to match cab profile, and EMD's typical cab with angled windshield glass.

The SDP40F was Amtrak's first new locomotive and seemed to provide the answer to their requirements for long-haul passenger locomotive. However, a spate of derailments, still unexplained to many, resulted in a loss of confidence, and they were replaced with the F40PH after only eight years of service. The Santa Fe took 18 in trade for some smaller utility locomotives and operated their SDP40Fs apparently without major problems. They were regeared for freight use, had front steps and platforms installed, and were redesignated SDF40-2s. In a second trip through the maintenance shops they had their noses notched to allow easier boarding. These are the only SDP40Fs in service.

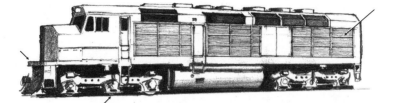

EMD F40C

EMD SDP40F
(Modified by Santa Fe)

EMD FP45

Length: 72 ft. 4 in. *Horsepower:* 3,600 *Cyl.:* 20
Date of mfr.: 1967–1968 *Approx. no. built:* 14

A rare and massive locomotive with a full-width hood over the engine platform, unusual for its time. Air inlets are along the top of the hood with the central intake just behind the cab, the dynamic-brake intakes halfway back (if the system is present), and three cooling radiator air intakes near the rear under the three fans. All the intakes are beveled with the roofline. There are two hood access doors on either side with portholes. A sizeable space extends aft of the radiators for the steam generator. Its exhaust stack was visible when the steam unit was still there. The cab with its angled windshield was a new design at the time, one that would be revived in the '80s with the wide-nose revolution. Note the huge fuel tank between the six-wheel Flexicoil trucks. Note also the road-switcher platforms at each end.

At the request of the Santa Fe, EMD produced this full-width version of the SDP45 (see page 56). Aesthetically, hood units left much to be desired, particularly on classy passenger trains like the Super Chief. The smooth sides took the warbonnet paint job well, cleaned up easier, and provided enclosed maintenance space. The Milwaukee Road ordered five, the only other railroad to use FP45s. All were converted to freight use when Amtrak took over nationwide passenger service. Some rosters are confusing regarding the designation, but at this time the Santa Fe operates the remaining eight FP45s as SDFP45s, numbered 90–98, excluding number 94.

EMD F45

Length: 63 ft. 3½ in. *Horsepower:* 3,600 *Cyl.:* 20
Date of mfr.: 1968–1971 *Approx. no. built:* 86

Closely resembles an FP45 but without the extra length behind the radiators. In fact it is basically an SD45 with the full-width hood. The fuel tank is noticeably shorter than on the FP45.

Designed from the beginning as a freight locomotive, the F45 was somewhat more successful than its passenger-hauling cousin, although few remain in service today. The Santa Fe has most of them, but as SDF45s. SDP40F was similar but had high-traction trucks and no portholes.

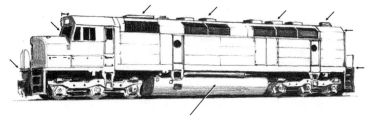

EMD FP45

EMD F45

EMD F40PH

Length: 56 ft. 2 in. *Horsepower:* 3,000/3,200 *Cyl.:* 16
Date of mfr.: 1976–1988 *Number built:* 375

A short, sloped-nosed locomotive with no front platform on Blomberg trucks, it will probably be seen pulling and pushing commuter trains. Most notable field mark is the featureless nose with an overbite extending forward past the pilot. Typical EMD full-width hood details, but cab and nose are shorter than in the earlier FP series and have trapezoid-shaped windshield glass, which is unique to EMD's F40 series. Avoid confusion with the earlier FP series by noting the cab's style. The various F40PHs are fairly common around Chicago, Boston, and other Amtrak cities on both coasts. Via in Canada has dozens.

Variables are mostly in the nomenclature and auxiliary electrical equipment. The F40PH-2 is virtually identical to the F40PH, and the F40PHR designates those F40PHs built from trade-in SDP40Fs. However, the 25 F40PH-2Cs, operated by the Massachusetts Bay Transportation Authority, are a noticeable 8 ft. longer with space for a head-end power unit aft of the radiators.

The F40PHM-2 — of which 30 were built for Metra (the Chicago Transit Authority) in 1992 and 1993 — has the windshield brought forward, giving it a distinctive European look, but is otherwise an F40PH variant.

Although small in number, commuter locomotives have high visibility, and I include a couple of interesting remanufacturing projects by Morrison Knudsen. The GP40FH-2 is the only full-width-hood locomotive in this book with a standard, road-switcher cab. Fourteen of these units operate around New York city for New Jersey Transit and Metro North. MK combined the F40PH hood and FP series cab to build five F40PHL-2s for Tri-Rail, a south Florida line between Miami and West Palm Beach. On the other side of the country, check North County Transit's F40PHM-2C Coaster out of San Diego.

FULL-WIDTH HOOD/B-B

EMD F40PH, F40PH-2, F40PHR

EMD F40PH-2C

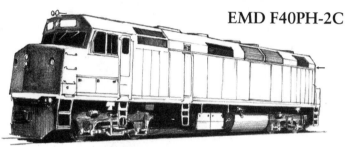

EMD F40PHM-2

MK-F40PHL-2

MK-GP40FH-2

EMD F59PH

Length: 58 ft. 2 in. *Horsepower:* 3,000 *Cyl.:* 12
Date of mfr.: 1988–present *Number built:* 65

Hard-edged replacement for the F40 series uses EMD's three-piece windshield cab design with front platform and familiar beveled hood. There are four rooftop cooling fans: one for the dynamic brakes, two for the prime mover's radiators, and one that appears to be for the head-end power unit. There are no small hood access doors and no portholes. The usual Blomberg trucks.

Essentially a GP59 with a full-width hood and head-end power, the F59PH has found some success in the new commuter locomotive market with Metrolink in California and GO Transit in Ontario. Others are bound to follow, and EMD's success with this type will apparently continue as there is no present competition other than remanufactured locomotives.

EMD F59PHI

Length: 58 ft. 2 in. *Horsepower:* 3,200 *Cyl.:* 12
Date of mfr.: 1994–present

Another GP59 with fancy bodywork, the F59PHI is unlikely to be confused with anything else. The bulbous new composite nose has a big three-piece windshield, and the hood is decorated with textured panels also made of composite materials. The rooftop hump is actually a curved scoop intended to lift the exhaust gases free of the following cars and to visually line up with them. Blomberg trucks, of course. Headlight is centered under the windshield and flanked by tough-to-read number boards (an early modification, I predict).

Main features of the F59PHI are its isolated cab (hence the initial *I*) to improve the crew's ride and acoustic environment, its low-emission engine, and a new microprocessor control. In California both Caltrans and Metrolink have placed orders, as has BC Transit in Vancouver.

Certainly a new approach to diesel styling, it remains to be seen how the notion of applying plastic panels for visual effect will withstand the realities of hard daily use. It is true that we have lived for a long time with a hard-edged, blocky look, from the first low-nosed "Geeps" to the latest AC4400CWs. Still, for all their brutal character, they are honest expressions of what they are: powerful, mobile, human-driven mechanical/electrical devices. It is interesting to compare the approach of the F59PHI designers with that of the AMD-103 Genesis (see next page), the other current attempt to break some new ground in diesel locomotive design.

FULL-WIDTH HOOD/B-B

EMD F59PH

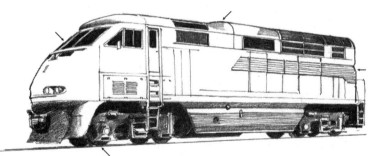

EMD F59PHI

GE AMD-103 (P40-BWH) Genesis, AMD-110(P32AC-DM)

Length: 69 ft. *Horsepower:* 4,000 *Cyl.:* 16
Date of mfr.: 1993–present *Number built:* 52

Unique, and only seen pulling Amtrak and Metro-North passenger trains. Extremely sleek monocoque body with a blunt, sliced-off nose that makes it appear very tall from the front. Fairly smooth roofline with a single large cooling fan at the rear. Radiator air intakes are low. Other air inlets are neatly arranged high along the side panels where the bodywork angles in. The windshield is curiously small, almost a slit across the nearly flat face. Headlights, number board, and even the side grabirons are flush fitted. Deep skirts streamline but also partly obscure the special radial-steering, high-tech trucks seen only on this locomotive.

The first really new approach to diesel locomotive design in decades, the Genesis is becoming a common sight at Amtrak stations. Handsome from the side but odd looking from the front, it has been likened to an inchworm. A 3,200-horsepower version with electrified third-rail pick-up gear is entering service at Penn Station and will replace the veteran FL9s in use there for nearly 40 years.

Nomenclature has been a problem, at least to us onlookers. "AMD-103," for Amtrak Diesel-103 mph, was used during development, and a contest resulted in the name Genesis. Factory and Amtrak designations have ranged from Dash-8-40BP and Dash-8-P40B to P40-BWH. Amtrak engineers simply call them P-40s. The Phase II, AMD-110 third-rail models are called P32AC-DM for passenger, 3,200 hp, AC traction motors and dual mode (diesel and electric). Unfortunately they are called P-32s for short, causing confusion with the earlier wide-nosed P32-8BWH units (see page 76). This will eventually settle out, but if you can see the locomotive numbers, the P-40s are the 800s, the similar P-32AC-DMs are in the 700s and the P32-8BWHs are 600s.

EMD F69PH-AC

Length: 58 ft. 2 in. *Horsepower:* 3,000 *Cyl.:* 12
Date of mfr.: 1989 *Number built:* 2

Now seen only at EMD's test facility, the F69PH-AC was built to promote EMD/Siemens AC traction equipment. At one time they appeared in Amtrak paint, but no sales were forthcoming and they are now back in their Siemens/Electro-Motive demo colors. They are mentioned here both to distinguish them from Metra's F40PHM-2 which, unlike the F69PH-AC, one is very likely to see in the Chicago area, and as another look at what may lie ahead in diesel locomotive design.

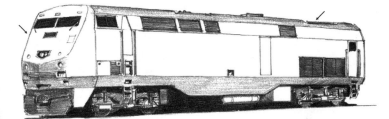

Genesis AMD-103

EMD F69PH-AC

EMD F series (F3, F7, F9)

Length: 50 ft. 8 in. *Horsepower:* 1,500 (F9, 1,750) *Cyl.:* 16
Date of mfr.: F3 1945–1949; F7 1949–1953; F9 1954–1957
Approx. no. built: F3 1,111; F7 2,366; F9 87

The familiar outline that defined American railroading for
decades continues to haul freight today, 50 years later. The F series' rounded contours look as fresh and lovely on the many re-
furbished units that continue to appear as they did in 1945. Easily identified, they can be confused with the six-axle E series
passenger units of the same era if you don't count the wheels or
notice the E's much greater length (see page 100). B units, unmanned boosters, of each model were also built in considerable
number, but fewer than 20 remain.

The F3 was originally recognizable by its two portholes and
the wire screening over the hood air intakes. Early F3s had tall
exhaust-fan shrouds, a third porthole, and a small rear hood
opening. Late F3s and F7s used a full-length grille over the high
openings and four sets of louvers instead of screened openings
between the portholes. The F9 refined the long grille, emphasiz-
ing the horizontal grid, and added a fifth set of louvers ahead of
the front porthole. These louvers eventually became simple,
square air filters. All three models have four roof fans and ride
on Blomberg trucks.

Perhaps a hundred of the units that put steam out of business
still rumble around the country, and *EXTRA 2200 South,* the
locomotive news magazine, often carries photographs of resurgent F units. Recent examples show off the handsome paint
schemes of the Colorado and Wyoming Railroad and the
Toledo, Peoria and Western. Several other F units are involved
with tourist railroads and dinner trains, a new enterprise that
helps keep some of our favorite machinery alive. They're out
there.

EMD FP7, FP9

Length: 54 ft. 8 in. *Horsepower:* FP7 1,500; FP9 1,750
Cyl.: 6 *Date of mfr.:* FP7 1949–1953; FP9 1954–1959
Number built: FP7 376; FP9 79

The FP7 and FP9 are basically stretched F7s and F9s, built especially for passenger service. The extra length allows space for a
steam generator and additional water supply. Note the extra
space between the first porthole and the first set of louvers on
the FP7. Also noticeable is the large gap between the front truck
and the battery box/fuel tank assembly. The FP9 has the first
porthole moved back and the first set of louvers installed just
ahead of it, making it harder to judge the FP9's added length.
Forty or so of both types are scattered widely in the U.S. and
Canada.

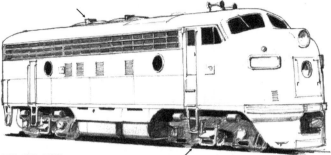

EMD F7

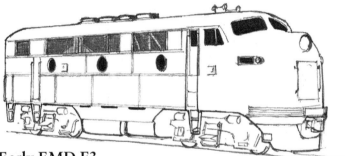

Early EMD F3

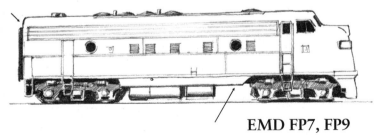

EMD FP7, FP9

EMD FL9

Length: 59 ft. *Horsepower:* 1,750–1,800 *Cyl.:* 16
Date of mfr.: 1956–1957 and 1960 *Number built:* 60

The distinguishing feature is obviously the six-axle, A1A Flexi-coil truck at the rear of the unit. Developed for and sold only to the New Haven railroad, the FL9 was able to run as a diesel locomotive or as an electric, capable of operation from two types of third-rail power pick-up. It is otherwise very similar to an FP9, with the extra length seen at the rear between the ladders.

The Connecticut Department of Transportation continues to operate ten FL9s, interestingly enough in the original New Haven paint scheme.

EMD E8, E9

Length: 70 ft. 3 in. *Horsepower:* E8 2,250; E9 2,400
Cyl.: 2 × 12 *Date of mfr.:* E8 1949–1953; E9 1954–1963
Number built: E8 421; E9 100

Nose is similar to the F series but unit is much longer and on six-axle trucks. Typically there are four portholes spaced along the side panels with a full-length grille above, although these items may vary. There are two exhaust stacks and two sets of four cooling fans, although two fans in each set seem always covered by winterization hatches. Number boards were originally flush with the nose contours. E8s and E9s are identical except for the headlight glass, which is recessed on the E8 but flush on the E9, unless they have been altered. Their predecessor, the E7, is now a museum piece but differed by having multiple rectangular openings in the side panels, projecting number boards, and a flush roofline. The suffix A as in E9A refers to the full cab locomotive, whereas E9B is the matching cabless booster unit.

Descended from a line of streamliners that began in 1937, only E8s and E9s survive outside of museums, most of them E9s. Long, twin-engined passenger locomotives, they are impressive sights running in sets with booster units. Union Pacific maintains such a set out of Cheyenne, Wyo., that is worth the trip to see. Their set is actually called upon occasionally to pull real trains, including freights. Conrail, Burlington Northern, and Amtrak also list them on their rosters. Another dozen or so are with small railroads and commuter lines across the country.

EMD FL9

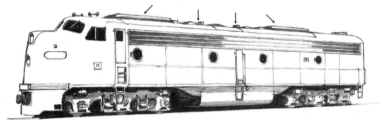

EMD E8A, E9A

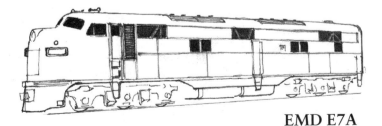

EMD E7A

Alco FA-1, FA-2

Length: 51 ft. 6 in. *Horsepower:* 1,500–1,600 *Cyl.:* 12
Date of mfr.: FA-1 1946–1950; FA-2 1950–1956
Number built: FA-1 432; FA-2 395

Similar in size to EMD's F series, Alco's FAs are huskier and more aggressive looking. Full-length air-intake screen with radiator shutters to the rear. The FA2 has the single large radiator fan and accompanying shutters moved forward, the only spotting feature that distinguishes the FA-1 and FA-2. Note the AAR-type trucks and the underframe clutter between them. There is an engine access door halfway back with a porthole.

Alco's first powerful diesel locomotive was rushed to the market to compete with EMD's FT and suffered serious teething problems with its untried engine. Still, production was significant although never threatening to EMD. A passenger version, the FPA-4 or FP4, was built in 1959 and 1960 by MLW for Canadian National only. They are recognizable by the additional air-intake area under the FA-2-type radiator shutters.

FAs are still in daily use on the Long Island Railroad but not as locomotives. They are towed along simply to provide head-end power for the passenger cars, and no doubt their days are numbered. Happily though, at least at this writing, you can still be pulled around by an FPA on the Western Maryland Scenic Railroad or even by a matched pair of FPAs on the Napa Valley Wine Train in California.

Alco PA-1, PA-2, PA-3

Length: 65 ft. 8 in. *Horsepower:* PA-1 2,000; PA-2, PA-3 2,250
Cyl.: 16 *Date of mfr.:* PA1 1946–1950; PA-2 1950–1952;
PA-3 1952–1953 *Approx. no. built:* PA-1 170; PA-2 28;
PA-3 49

A handsome long nose on a long chassis riding on extra-long trucks gives an impression of power and speed. Looking like a stretched FA, the PA has similar detailing: single large cooling fan, and a flat roof and nose with the top headlight embedded in grillework. Radiator shutters interrupt the window-level air intakes. PA-3s lack the automobile-like trim over the cab side windows and the porthole aft of the radiator shutters.

Initially plagued with mechanical problems, as were its cousins the FAs, the PAs went on to become common sights on major railroads for 20 years after their introduction.

Possibly a couple of PA-1s are still alive in Mexico amid rumors of one being rebuilt. Another sits in a Mexican museum. The others' fates are unknown to me, but they appear to have been scrapped. Surely there is a derelict parked somewhere that could be rebuilt to pull a dinner train or a tourist excursion.

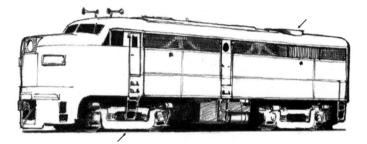

Alco FA-1, FA-2

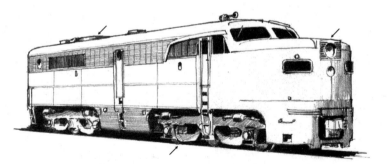

Alco PA-1, PA-2, PA-3

EMD BL2

Length: 54 ft. *Horsepower:* 1,500 *Cyl.:* 16
Date of mfr.: 1948–1949 *Number built:* 58

Unmistakable, but extremely rare, soon to be found only in railroad museums. Most obvious features are the sculpted side panels intended to provide better visibility from the cab when switching than did their contemporary, full-bodied road diesels. The cab is somewhat related visually to EMD's F series, but with a longer nose and large windows. From windowsill height the hood is sloped, softening the visual impact of the high sides. There are four radiator cooling fans centered between the windshield and the sloping rear hood line. Modelers have identified a couple of phases of BL2 production based on pilot details and an extra set of louvers in the cheeks just forward of the cab. Units equipped for passenger service with steam generator in the nose had an exhaust-stack housing rising between the windshields.

Resisting the look of typical road switchers that were appearing from Baldwin, Alco, and Fairbanks-Morse, EMD designers came up with this curious blend of automobile styling and railroad engineering to house F3 mechanical gear. Although intended for general branch-line work, the BL2 was more an attempt to survey the locomotive market to determine the railroads' wants and needs. Few were sold, and EMD shortly began the long series of "Geeps" that would establish EMD as the premier builder of road switchers for some time to come. Even though unsuccessful in sales, the BL2's singular appearance and perceived role as the transition between cab and hood units (between F and GP series) has insured its place in hearts and history. The Bangor and Aroostook Railroad, an original purchaser, has only recently retired their last two units, and current rosters indicate only one or two running anywhere. Check tiny Stourbridge Railroad's enginehouse in Honesdale, Pa., or the South Branch Valley Railroad out of Moorefield, W. Va., but hurry.

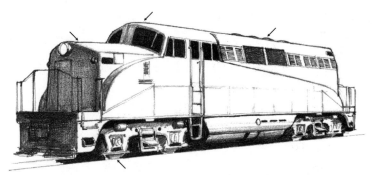

EMD BL2

The "Draper Taper"

Grouped together here are several distinct locomotives that share the same unique bodywork. Around 1980, Canadian National Railway's William L. Draper, assistant chief of motive power, designed full-width bodywork for the HR616, a Bombardier, Inc. locomotive evolved from earlier Montreal Locomotive Works and Alco models. His design featured a narrowing of the hood just aft of the cab that permitted better rearward visibility for the crew but still provided covered access to the engine. Later, Canadian National, BC Rail, and the Quebec North Shore and Labrador would order locomotives from EMD and GE, specifying Draper's hood design. Combined with the specified Comfort Cab, the "Draper Taper" lent a similar look to very different locomotives, all in Canada.

Bombardier, Inc. HR616

Length: 69 ft. 6 in. *Horsepower:* 3,000 *Cyl.:* 16
Date of mfr.: 1982 *Approx. no. built:* 20

Typical Canadian National style full-bodied locomotive on six-axle Montreal Locomotive Works trucks. Angled fuel tanks with two air reservoirs on the left side only. Smooth rooftop. Cab is early Canadian Comfort Cab with four-piece windshield. Outer panes droop. Of the several "Draper Taper" designs, only the HR616 has the recessed side entries just behind the cab near large panels of louvers. There are also large, nearly full-height radiator air intakes at the rear.

All 20 of the single original order are still in operation with Canadian National Railways.

GE C40-8M

Length: 71 ft. 8 in. *Horsepower:* 4,000 *Cyl.:* 16
Date of mfr.: 1990–1994 *Number built:* 84

Angular fuel tank eliminates EMD Draper designs, while high radiator air inlets with the newer Comfort Cab eliminates HR616. The rear intakes vary from side to side. Number boards and classification lights are nose mounted. Cab is virtually identical to EMD units. As with all CN's units, the paint job obscures the smooth lines of the C40-8M.

With this latest locomotive to sport the Draper bodywork, GE has found success north of the border, supplying them in number to Canadian National and BC Rail, with a few to the Quebec, North Shore and Labrador Railroad. It will be interesting to see if the Draper body can or will be adapted to the new top-of-the-line units from GE and EMD.

FULL-WIDTH HOOD/DRAPER/C-C

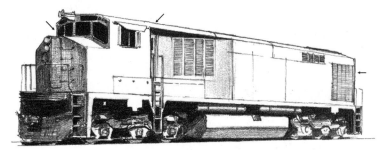

Bombardier HR616

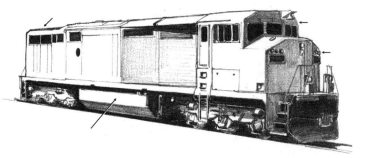

GE C40-8M

EMD SD50F

Length: 71 ft. 2 in. *Horsepower:* 3,600 *Cyl.:* 16
Date of mfr.: 1985–1987 *Number built:* 60

EMD's version of the Draper design uses the later Comfort Cab style with somewhat rounded corners and a higher roof with the four-piece windshield lined up. Entry to the cab is from outward-facing doors just behind the cab side windows. The roofline is broken up with typical EMD bumps and boxes, plus the usual three roof fans (a winterization hatch always covers the forward fan). The three radiators are mounted on a slant behind fine screening high on the hood sides at the rear. Standard EMD curved fuel tank is a certain field mark. All are in service with Canadian National Railways.

EMD SD60F

Length: 71 ft. 2 in. *Horsepower:* 3,800 *Cyl.:* 16
Date of mfr.: 1985–1989 *Number built:* 64

Nearly identical to the SD50F, but a few nose details will distinguish the SD60F from its forebears. Number boards and classification lights have been moved from high on the cab to the nose, and a louver has appeared in the cab access steps on the left side only. Even more subtle is the revised bell mounting bracket.

The 645 series engine had reached its limit of horsepower increases and the 710 series power plant of greater displacement was introduced (for Canadian National) in the SD60F along with computer-controlled wheel slip and control systems.

EMD SD40-2F

Length: 68 ft. 10 in. *Horsepower:* 3,000 *Cyl.:* 16
Date of mfr.: 1988 *Number built:* 25

Only in CP Rail colors, the SD40-2F has a two-part radiator grille rather than the three on SD50Fs and SD60Fs, which accounts for their additional length. Note the lack of cab access on the right side, but note also the hood access doors with portholes. Fuel tank is interestingly notched for steps. Three cooling fans, one covered by a winterization hatch.

Nearly three years after the last U.S.-built SD40-2, GM's London, Ont., plant produced 25 SD40-2Fs for Canadian Pacific, the only buyer of this model.

FULL-WIDTH HOOD/DRAPER/C-C

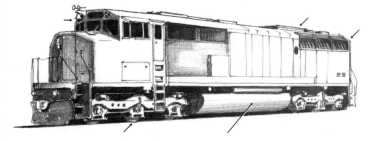

EMD SD50F

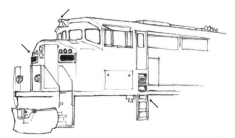

EMD SD60F

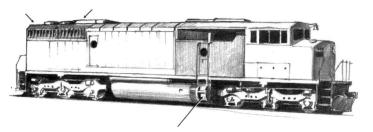

EMD SD40-2F

EMD AEM7

Length: 51 ft. 5¾ in. *Horsepower:* 7,000
Date of mfr.: 1979–1988 *Number built:* 67

Stubby, slab sided and double ended. Electrical pick-up and air conditioning equipment lines the roof, and a pantograph reaches up to the electric power lines. Sides are windowless, except for the cab, and corrugated. The two large-wheeled trucks are hidden under deep side skirts.

Fastest locomotive in North America, the AEM7 (or the "Toaster," as it is sometimes called because of its simple, boxy shape) is based on a Swedish design and was built under license by EMD for use along the Northeast Corridor from Washington, D.C., to New Haven (where the electrification stops). Look for most of them pulling fast passenger trains for Amtrak between New York and Washington. A few are in local commuter service between Wilmington, Philadelphia, and Trenton, and between Washington and Baltimore. Although Amtrak continues to look at high-speed trainsets for the future, the natural longevity of electric locomotives insures they will be around for a long while. "A" stands for the Swedish company ASEA, "EM" for EMD, and "7" for the 7,000 horsepower.

ABB ALP44

Length: 51 ft. 2 in. *Horsepower:* 7,000
Date of mfr.: 1990–1991 *Number built:* 33

Very close to the AEM7 in appearance, the ALP44 has differently styled grilles along the top, hiding electrical gear, and a simpler-looking pantograph. So far only in New Jersey Transit paint, they may soon be seen on the Southeast Pennsylvania Transit Authority's (SEPTA) tracks.

Designers of Amtrak's AEM7 (EMD built them under license), ABB Traction Inc. now markets a line of electric locomotives and commuter rail products directly to U.S. buyers. They have also remanufactured FL9s (now FL9-ACs) for Metro North Commuter Railroad of New York state, thus helping to keep the F series cab units in view.

EMD AEM7

ABB ALP44

EMD E60CP, E60CH
Length: 71 ft. 3 in. *Horsepower:* 6,000
Date of mfr.: 1974–1975 *Number built:* 26

A long, double-ended, windowless locomotive on massive six-axle trucks. Windshield notched into the blunt nose(s). Fairly smooth beveled roofline with slanted grilles amidships. Smooth sides with large water tanks slung between the trucks. Pantographs.

Adapted from an industrial mining locomotive, the E60CP was intended to replace the 40-year-old GG1s on Amtrak's high-speed Northeast Corridor runs. Derailments were a problem, however, and their top speed was capped, limiting their usefulness as passenger haulers. They were soon relegated to pulling heavy, long-distance trains at reduced speeds, while the AEM7 took over the high-speed runs. A dozen or so remain but will soon be phased out.

The E60CH is similar but has a head-end power alternator rather than a steam generator for electric instead of steam heat for passenger cars. The E60CH thus lacks the square housing at the roof just behind the cab and has battery boxes in lieu of water tanks. In 1982 and 1983 a similar but somewhat sleeker model, the E60C-2 was sold to National Railways of Mexico but had to await the electrification of routes out of Mexico City. A pair also operate between a Rangely, Colo., coal mine and a Bonanza, Utah, power station.

EMD GF6C

Length: 68 ft. 10 in. *Horsepower:* 6,000
Date of mfr.: 1983–1984 *Number built:* 7

Big, handsome, single cab (not double ended), full-width body locomotive restricted to an 80-mile electrified branch line in the northeast corner of British Columbia. Depressed roof holds pantographs, insulators, and switchgear. Nose is blunt but slightly pointed. The cab has a three-piece windshield and no front porch. Rolls on typical EMD road-switcher trucks.

Built for the sole purpose of hauling coal for the Japanese steel industry out of a remote wilderness area that had abundant, nearby hydroelectric power, the GF6C is ideally suited for sustained slow speeds and long tunnels. Ease of maintenance, low energy costs, and the fact that fewer units would be needed (compared to diesels), overcame higher initial cost as a deciding factor when setting up the railroad. The GF6C is a very desirable addition to your life list, but if you haven't been to British Columbia, you haven't seen one.

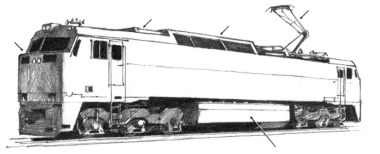

EMD E60CP, E60CH

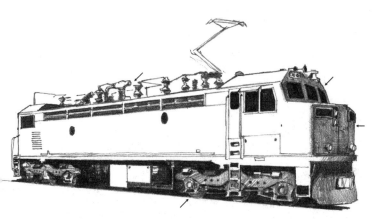

EMD GF6C

GE E44

Length: 69 ft. 6 in. *Horsepower:* 4,400–5,000
Date of mfr.: 1960–1963 *Number built:* 66

The E44 looks at first like a diesel road switcher with a cut-down cab, but the pantograph of course gives it away. It has a blunt, sloped nose, and high skirts along the hood hide electrical gear. It travels on trimount, three-motor trucks with uneven axle spacing.

Now relegated to utility work for Amtrak, the E44 was intended for heavy freight operation on the Pennsylvania Railroad's electrified lines that ran from New York to Washington and from Philadelphia to Harrisburg.

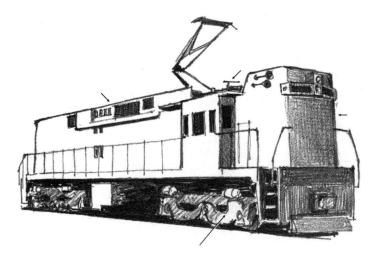

GE E44

Trainsets

Rarely mentioned in railroad literature are trainsets, strings of specially designed, lightweight, semipermanently coupled passenger cars, typically with a powered car at each end. Some might call them locomotives, so I have mentioned them here. Successful in Europe, the idea has not caught on in North America, where ridership of passenger trains is much less predictable, thus making it difficult to settle on an efficient train length.

Still, from time to time some of our railroads have experimented with the idea, and despite disappointing results, Amtrak and Via Rail of Canada operate lightweight trainsets on specific routes.

Via Rail uses the diesel-powered, Canadian-built (1980–1984) LRC (not "light-rail car" but "light, rapid, and comfortable," which translates easily into French) operating between Montreal and Toronto. Amtrak experimented with the French ANF turbine-powered Turboliner, then bought several sets built under license in the U.S. in 1976 by the Rohr Company, which is no longer in the trainset business. Amtrak uses the Rohr Turboliners only on the fairly predictable runs from Niagara Falls and Buffalo through Albany to New York City. They are equipped with third-rail shoes and electric motors for operation into Penn Station. The original French ANF trains are still on Amtrak's roster but are rarely seen. They can be told from the Rohr trains by their European twin headlights and a less-streamlined nose.

Despite their rarity, these unusual passenger trains are included here because of their high visibility. As intriguing as they are, it is likely that they will fade from our railroad scene. Without roadbed improvements to take advantage of their higher speeds, it is hard to justify the reputed high maintenance costs and the inflexibility of fixed-length trainsets.

LRC

Rohr Turboliner

Passenger Cars

There isn't a whole lot to write about when it comes to passenger service on U.S. railroads. Amtrak continues to struggle against a political mind-set that looks for immediate and consistent profits rather than long-term investment opportunities in operating a passenger rail system, despite the well-documented public interest in maintaining a good system nationwide. As a result, the U.S. continues to lag well behind Japanese and European passenger rail in technology and service. New trainsets, mostly European, are tried out regularly, stirring hopes, but are returned once the costs of improving roadbeds and straightening curves are added up.

Still, one can get a fine train ride across the country with a reasonable expectation of an on-time arrival and friendly personal service on generally clean and comfortable equipment. In 1970, when Amtrak was created to operate the country's passenger trains, the available equipment came from railroads all over the country, still decked out in their own paint jobs. Amtrak trains were colorful indeed if a little disharmonious. These Heritage cars, mostly dating from the '40s and '50s, were rebuilt and used until Amtrak's first new equipment, the Amfleet series, built by Budd, was delivered in the mid-'70s. For a time trains consisted of mixed Amfleet and Heritage cars. In the early '80s, bilevel Superliners were ordered to replace the hi-level Heritage cars originally from the Santa Fe and used only in the West. Amtrak's newest car, the Horizon, was built by the Bombardier company of Canada in 1989 and 1990. A new line of Viewliners built by MK Rail began service in 1995.

(I have not attempted to cover the gray area between street cars and passenger trains called commuter rail. This passenger equipment is often specially designed for each purchase and thus unique to a particular city.)

Despite its political problems, Amtrak does seem to have staying power, and the outpouring of public and local political support during the frantic federal budget cutting of 1995 was promising. Perhaps we can still have a real passenger rail system.

Heritage Fleet

The classic American streamliner. Flat sides with a rounded roofline, the Heritage cars are coaches, dome cars, food-service cars, and sleepers, and the oldest cars on Amtrak. Windows are single paned, and the eaves are textured with a finer corrugation than the fluting below the window line. The hi-level Heritage fleet, the ex–Santa Fe cars, had a dropped section between the trucks (necessary to make two levels) and a single entry midway along the fluted sides. The texturing continued above and below. The windows were divided into two panes.

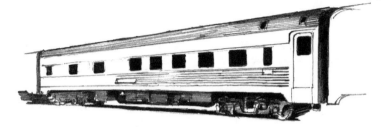

Heritage

Amfleet

Superliners

Resembling the hi-level Heritage cars, the equally tall Superliners are not as rounded and have many detail differences. Note the square-cut wheel openings, the bent central entry door, and the large louvered opening at one end. The two-piece windows are in continuous, flat, not corrugated, panels. The cars are configured as coaches, diners, lounge cars, and sleepers and used only in the West.

Amfleet Cars

With the graceful rounded fuselage, the single-level Amfleet cars look as though they owe something to the aircraft industry. Note the long, thin, two-paned windows and the simple (looking) four-wheel trucks. The horizontal fluted texture runs below the windows and carries up over the top as well. The first series, the Amfleet I, has a vestibule at each end. They come in coach and food-service versions. The Amfleet II series has a single vestibule and comes as a lounge car as well. The Amfleet cars are commonly used on eastern, short-haul trains.

Horizon Fleet

Sleek cars with small windows and slab sides that look as though they were extruded from a single bar of aluminum. Built in coach form only with an occasional food-service car, the Horizons are short haul, high-density seating, and a bit spartan inside as well as out. They are often used on commuter lines.

Viewliners

The Viewliners are intended to replace the aging Heritage cars on long-haul eastern trains. At first glance they may look like Superliners, but they're not as tall (to clear tight eastern bridges). Diners, coaches, and sleepers, they show two rows of windows and an end vestibule. There is no skirting between the trucks. The lower sides are ribbed and angle inward below the windows.

Horizon

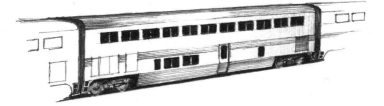

Superliner

Flatcars

The first freight car was no doubt a flatcar; simply a platform on which to place a load that needed to be moved. Today, various flatcar designs haul everything from farm machinery to shipping containers. It may seem unnecessary to describe a flatcar, as its name is virtually self-explanatory and its shape is so obvious. However there are many types of flatcars, and in recent times much innovative thought has gone into developing the flatcar for particular uses. The advent of widespread *piggybacking* (the loading of truck trailers onto flatcars) in the 1950s led to modifications of flatcars to better suit the hauling of truck trailers. Eventually special railroad cars were developed specifically for intermodal service.

Next came the extended 54-ft. flatcar fitted with hitches, tie-downs, and rub rails, that could carry two trailers, followed by still longer cars up to 89 ft., and now special designs such as the minimal spine car, basically a beam on wheels with hitches and small truck-wheel platforms to secure the road trailer. They are available individually or in permanently coupled multiple units that share sets of wheels where the units join. Well cars can carry a double stack of standard containers by dropping a container down between the side rails, supported by edge- and crossbeams. A second container is stacked on top. Although no longer resembling flat cars, these special applications are derived from the original simple concept of hauling something out in the open where it is easy to load and unload.

Other developments are the bulkhead flatcars that secure loads longitudinally and the interesting centerbeam cars that not only provide a convenient barrier to load lumber and building supplies against, but are significantly strengthened thus allowing heavier loads. Although similar in some ways to boxcars, auto carriers are basically long flatcars fitted with a perforated shroud protecting three levels of new cars from vandalism and weather. The depressed-center flatcar carries higher, heavier loads. Coiled steel sheets are hauled on special flatcars equipped with removable hoods.

Many other variations can be seen hauling a variety of cargo, making the flatcar perhaps the most interesting freight car to the trainwatcher.

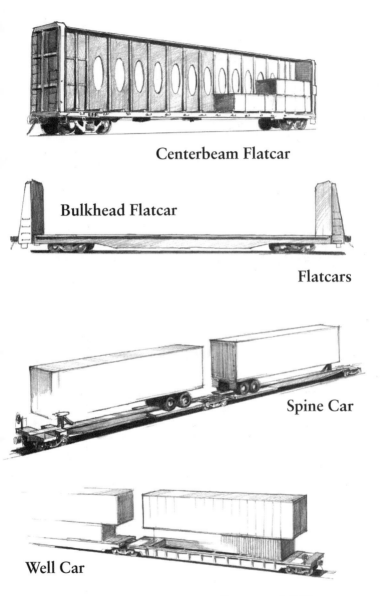

Centerbeam Flatcar

Bulkhead Flatcar

Flatcars

Spine Car

Well Car

Intermodal Flatcars

Gondolas

After the plain flatcar the gondola is the simplest, most basic hauler of just about anything that can take the weather. It originated in the 1870s as a replacement for the small coal jimmies, and in coal service it soon evolved a drop-bottom that led to the later hopper cars. Today it hauls bulk cargo as well as crated shipments, steel products, and pipe, to name only a few of its loads. It is often seen on sidings loaded with scrap metal and looking very beat up.

The typical gondola is solid bottomed and low sided for easier loading, but variations come in several heights, with tall wood chip gondolas looking like doorless boxcars. Some are equipped for rotary dumping; that is, the car is unloaded by machines that roll it over while the car stays coupled to the train with special rotary couplers. Some gondolas are covered. Varying in length from 40 to 70 ft., they are still built in large numbers today.

Hoppers

The most common type of freight car since about 1980, the hopper comes in various shapes and sizes. All are recognizable as hoppers, however, by the visible discharge gates underneath. Originally developed for coal, stone, and ore hauling, the open-top hopper still carries great quantities of coal in 100-car trains from coal fields to power plants. In fact, it is coal hauling that is largely responsible for the resurgent rail freight business in recent years, requiring not only more hopper cars but new and more efficient diesel engines to pull them (as described elsewhere in this book). The declining interest in nuclear power and the increasing demand for electricity resulted in the hopper displacing the boxcar as the most numerous freight car.

Covered hoppers continue to evolve and now carry not only grain and cement but plastic pellets, chemical granules, powders, food products, and even garbage. This wide variety of materials requires innovative designs and sophisticated materials to avoid contamination while maintaining efficient handling. Stainless steel, aluminum, and fiberglass are employed in these often sleek and handsome cars. Some are of conventional outside-braced construction. Others are smooth sided and nearly cylindrical. A string of hoppers can usually be found at a grain elevator or a plastics manufacturer.

FREIGHT CARS

Gondola

HOPPERS

Open-topped Hopper

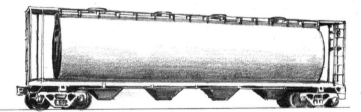

Cylindrical Covered Hopper

Covered Hopper

Boxcars

Easily recognizable with their side-opening doors, boxcars are as common as they are variable. The classic 40-footer with its handsome "dreadnought" stamped ends has given way to a variety of longer, taller, more sophisticated designs with far greater capacity. Ranging from 50 to 90 ft. long and from 70 to 100 tons of capacity, boxcars still haul a great variety of goods, even though covered hoppers and intermodal flatcar trains have taken over some of the specialized cargo formerly shipped by boxcar.

Interior load restraints such as movable bulkheads, end cushioning, and even air bags have greatly improved efficiency and damage prevention. Specially insulated, precooled cars carry perishables not needing mechanical refrigeration as well as cargos sensitive to condensation. Refrigerated boxcars now use carbon dioxide "snow" to maintain frozen meats, juice, and other products. Huge boxcars specially developed for shipping car parts roll toward auto assembly plants around the country to be unloaded through multiple wide doors. Slatted, 90-ft. livestock cars carry up to 120 animals on two decks.

Welcome to railfans is the renewed emphasis on colorful graphics seen on many rail cars, particularly the new reefers with their company logos, a practice not common since the steam era.

Tank Cars

Today, the familiar cylindrical shape can contain a great variety of liquids and gases in contrast to an earlier time in the 20th century when petroleum was the principal commodity carried by tanker. The ensuing industrial and agricultural development created a need for specialized cars for such varied liquid materials as acids, polymers, and other chemicals for industry, and fertilizers, vegetable oils, fruit juices, and wines for agricultural use. Compressed gases such as propane, carbon dioxide, and anhydrous ammonia are major cargos of tank car trains.

Tank cars range in length from 30 to 65 ft. but are limited by regulation to a capacity of 34,500 gallons. Visually they are just a tank with wheels under each end. An interesting variant is the "Funnel Flow" tanker which is slightly sloped toward the middle from each end, giving it a bent appearance, but allowing it to be drained by gravity.

The large number of commodities classified as hazardous has resulted in regulations concerning tank car design and use. Included are structural requirements and temperature regulation by insulation and heating coils. Little of this is evident from the outside however, and the tank car has, if anything, become even simpler and more elegant in appearance over time.

Boxcars

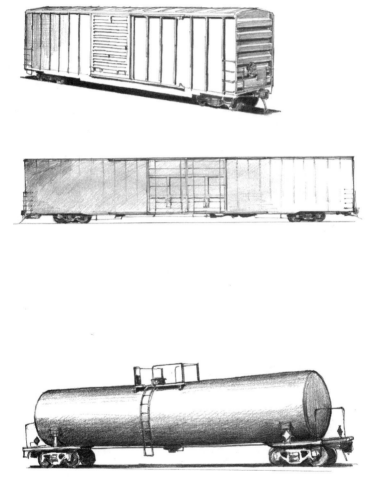

54-ft. Funnel-Flow Tank Car

Caboose

Disappearing everywhere, the caboose is nevertheless a nostalgic favorite. After defining the end of the train for over a century, it is being replaced by a gadget — the *End of Train Device* — that can be hung on the last freight car and monitor brake-line pressure while blinking its light. Hardly a worthy substitute for an institution in American folklore, but advances in electronics and communications have made the caboose unnecessary, at least on large railroads.

The last cabooses made, those one is likely to come across, fell into three basic types: the cupola, with a raised observation roost; the bay-window type with slight projections on either side; and the wide-vision model, which is really a wide cupola model, with the cupola extending over the sides. Each railroad had its preferred configuration and most built their own with special cabooses sometimes built for specific uses. Cabooses are commonly thought to be red but in fact were often painted for their railroad's colors: black, green, yellow, and blue to name a few.

Cabooses functioned as the conductor's office, a temporary home for the crew, tool shack, and refuge from the elements and the locomotive. They were equipped with stoves for cooking and heating, bunks, lockers, and a desk. Some late versions had plumbing, electricity, radio communications, and even air conditioning.

Train lore is filled with caboose stories, both comedies and tragedies, but as Lucious Beebe wrote in the last line of his classic, *Highball,* "The saga of the high iron would be the poorer had they never been."

Caboose

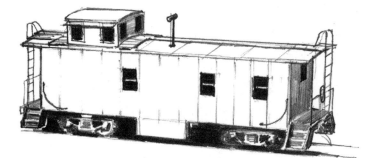

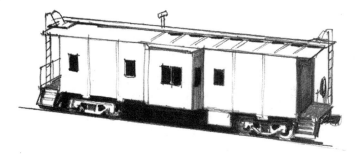

Glossary

A unit A manned diesel locomotive with crew cab and operating controls. This is distinguished from the matching but unmanned B or booster unit.

AAR The Association of American Railroads, which is concerned with industry standards and the promotion of railroad interests.

Adhesion The frictional grip of wheels on the rail.

B unit A cabless, matching diesel locomotive designed as a booster to A units. B units were primarily associated with the EMD F series and Alco PA locomotives, but there are current examples such as the B units supporting Santa Fe's GP60Ms and Burlington Northern's B30-7 boosters.

Battery box A louvered box housing storage batteries for starting the engine and powering accessories when the engine is not running. They are usually seen along the walkway near the cab.

Blower duct The duct carrying air from the central equipment blower to cool the traction motors, particularly noticeable on EMD locomotives.

Bulk freight Loose loads such as gravel, coal, grain, and plastic pellets, usually hauled in hopper cars.

Catenary The cable system of overhead conductors providing electrical power from an outside source to electric locomotives.

Comfort cab A larger locomotive cab with a full-width nose to improve crew comfort (and efficiency). It was originally known as the Canadian Cab, having been first specified on Canadian railroads.

COFC An acronym for Container On Flatcar, indicating the loading of standard shipping containers on specially equipped flat cars.

Coupler In this book the AAR standard device for connecting locomotives and railroad cars together; manually opened but automatically locked when pushed together.

Diesel Commonly a diesel locomotive, but more precisely the compression-ignition type of internal combustion engine.

Diesel-electric The more accurate name for a diesel locomotive referring to the generation of electricity by a diesel engine, the prime mover.

Dynamic braking The locomotive braking system utilizing the kinetic energy of the train's movement to generate electric current at the traction motors to slow the train. The resulting excess heat is dissipated through banks of resistor grids cooled by fans.

Electric locomotive A self-propelled locomotive utilizing electric motors to drive wheels. Unlike diesel-electric locomotives that generate their own power, electricity is obtained from overhead lines (catenary) or an additional (third) rail.

Grille Opening for an air intake on diesel locomotives protected by wire mesh or similar grating assembly.

HEP or Head-End-Power Separate electric power generated by a locomotive's prime mover to provide for lighting, heating, and air-conditioning on passenger trains.

High-adhesion truck Locomotive truck designed to enhance wheel-rail contact.

Micro-processor control Computer monitoring and control of the prime mover and auxiliary electrical equipment, such as cooling fans, in the interest of greater efficiency.

Pantograph On an electric locomotive the flexible rooftop assembly reaching to the overhead catenary for electric power.

Piggy-back The method of transporting highway trailers and containers on flatcars.

Prime mover On a diesel locomotive, the central diesel power plant that generates electricity for the traction motors and auxiliary equipment.

Push-pull The back and forth operation of commuter trains without uncoupling the locomotive and moving it to the "front." The train can be operated from either end by the installation of controls in the last car.

Reservoir The cylindrical tanks containing compressed air for operation of air brake cylinders.

Short haul Moving a train a shorter than maximum distance on a given railroad.

Shortline A railroad with less than a hundred miles of mainline track.

Slug An unmanned diesel locomotive with traction motors only operating from the prime mover of the manned locomotive it is attached to.

TOFC Acronym for Trailer On Flatcar, the transporting of highway truck trailers by train.

Third rail The extra rail outside the running rails that provides power through a pick-up shoe on electric locomotives.

Traction motor The axle-mounted electric motor that drives the associated wheels on diesel and electric locomotives.

Trucks The sets of wheels, including axles, frames, and suspension under each end of diesel and electric locomotives, and freight and passenger cars. They are usually two-axle (four-wheel) trucks or three-axle (six-wheel) trucks.

Turbocharger An exhaust-driven blower that supercharges the prime mover.

Unit train A train carrying one commodity from its source to its destination as with a coal train hauling coal from the mine to the power plant.

Wheel-slip control A system that senses wheel slippage, controls power to the wheel, and provides sanding automatically.

Life List

____ABB ALP44
____Alco C-420
____Alco C-424
____Alco C-425
____Alco C-430
____Alco C-628
____Alco C-630
____Alco C-636
____Alco FA-1
____Alco FA-2
____Alco PA-1
____Alco PA-2
____Alco PA-3
____Alco RS1
____Alco RS2
____Alco RS3
____Alco RS11
____Alco RSD12
____Alco RSD15
____Alco S-1
____Alco S-2
____Alco S-3
____Alco S-4
____Alco S-6
____Alco T-6
____Baldwin Road Switcher Series
____Baldwin VO 1000
____Baldwin DS-4-4-10
____Baldwin S-12
____Bombardier, Inc. HR616
____EMD AEM7
____EMD (AT&SF) CF7
____EMD BL2
____EMD DD40AX Centennial
____EMD E8
____EMD E9
____EMD E60CH

____EMD E60CP
____EMD F3
____EMD F7
____EMD F9
____EMD F40C
____EMD F40PH
____EMD F45
____EMD F59PH
____EMD F59PHI
____EMD F69PH-AC
____EMD FL9
____EMD FP7
____EMD FP9
____EMD FP45
____EMD GF6C
____EMD GMD1
____EMD GP7
____EMD GP9
____EMD GP15-1
____EMD GP18
____EMD GP20
____EMD GP30
____EMD GP35
____EMD GP38-2
____EMD GP38-2W
____EMD GP39
____EMD GP40
____EMD GP40-2
____EMD GP50
____EMD GP59
____EMD GP60
____EMD GP60M
____EMD MP15(DC)
____EMD MP15AC
____EMD MP15T
____EMD NW2
____EMD RS1325
____EMD SD7
____EMD SD9
____EMD SD18
____EMD SD24
____EMD SD35
____EMD SD38
____EMD SD38-2
____EMD SD39
____EMD SD40
____EMD SD40-2
____EMD SD40-2F
____EMD SD40-2(W)
____EMD SD40T-2
____EMD SD45

_____EMD SD45-2
_____EMD SD45T-2
_____EMD SD50
_____EMD SD50F
_____EMD SD60
_____EMD SD60F
_____EMD SD60I
_____EMD SD60M
_____EMD SD60MAC
_____EMD SD70
_____EMD SD70MAC
_____EMD SD75M
_____EMD SD80MAC
_____EMD SD90MAC
_____EMD SDL39
_____EMD SDP35
_____EMD SDP40F
_____EMD SW1
_____EMD SW7
_____EMD SW9
_____EMD SW8
_____EMD SW600
_____EMD SW900
_____EMD SW1000
_____EMD SW1001
_____EMD SW1200
_____EMD SW1500
_____EMD SW1504
_____Fairbanks-Morse H-12-
    44
_____GE AC600 CW
_____GE AC4400CW
_____GE AMD-103 (P40-
    BWH) Genesis
_____GE AMD-110 (P32AC-
    DM) Genesis
_____GE/AT&SF SF30C
_____GE B23-7
_____GE B30-7
_____GE B30-7A
_____GE B30-7A1
_____GE B32-8
_____GE B32-8WH(P32-
    8BWH)
_____GE B36-7
_____GE B39-8
_____GE B40-8
_____GE B40-8W
_____GE BQ23-7
_____GE C30-7
_____GE C30-7A

____GE C32-8
____GE C36-7
____GE C39-8
____GE C39-8E
____GE C40-8
____GE C40-8M
____GE C40-8W
____GE C40-9
____GE C41-8W
____GE C44-9W
____GE E44
____GE U18B
____GE U23B
____GE U23C
____GE U25B
____GE U25C
____GE U28B
____GE U28C
____GE U30B
____GE U30C
____GE U33B
____GE U33C
____GE U36B
____GE U36C
____MLW M420(W)
____MLW M420R
____MLW S-13
____Morrison Knudsen
____MK1200G
____Morrison Knudsen
____MK5000C

____ _____
____ _____
____ _____
____ _____
____ _____
____ _____
____ _____
____ _____
____ _____
____ _____
____ _____
____ _____
____ _____
____ _____
____ _____
____ _____
____ _____
____ _____
____ _____

Acknowledgments and Further Reading

As I look around my studio at the stacks of books and periodicals I referred to while researching this *Field Guide to Trains,* I am keenly aware of the efforts of those who wrote and researched before me. Their detailed investigations into all the corners of railroading are of great value to us all. As those writers well know, railroad writing is particularly a work of love.

In that light, the good effort put in by so many enthusiasts is simply astonishing and I am grateful for their work. The best way for me to thank them is to underline their importance and recommend their works to others. Of particular value to me are the series of *Contemporary Diesel Spotters Guides* by Louis Marre and Jerry Pinkepank, and Charles McDonald's *Diesel Locomotive Rosters.* James Kerr's annual *Locomotive Rosters and News* was essential. No enthusiast's library is complete without these works.

Among periodicals *Diesel Era,* with its thorough analysis of equipment, and *Extra 2200 South's* timely reporting on diesel locomotive matters are eagerly awaited each quarter. *Mainline Modeler* and *Model Railroader* supply detailed information from the modeler's point of view. *Trains* and *Railfan* keep us aware of the contemporary scene while mixing in a little nostalgia and folklore. There are many others.

John H. White's work certainly exemplifies the best in railroad literature. His two works, *The American Railroad Passenger Car* and *The American Railroad Freight Car* are graduate courses in railroad history; exhaustive and comprehensive yet highly readable. Bob Haydon's *Diesel Locomotive Cyclopedia* is an invaluable reference. Even the *Walther's HO Catalog* was helpful. But again, there are many more good books than I can name here.

Manufacturers were generously forthcoming with information only they can provide. In particular, EMD's photo lab at LaGrange, Illinois, was most helpful in settling many puzzles for me while answering what must have often seemed strange questions. MK Rail enthusiastically furnished me with photos and articles fully describing their operation and products.

Thanks go to my good friend and neighbor, noted author M. R. Montgomery, for his sound advice and counsel that helped me keep my task in focus.

A project such as this is one of constant refinement, and the process continues as more information develops and becomes available. I anticipate and welcome the comments and critique of railfans, the railroad enthusiasts who keep alive the formal and informal information networks that instruct us in all the various workings of the railroad industry, past and present. More than any other reward I want this book to be a service to them.

Index

ABB ALP44, 110
AC4400CW, GE, 84
AC6000CW, GE, 84
AEM7, EMD, 110
Alco C-420, 26
Alco C-424, 40
Alco C-425, 40
Alco C-430, 40
Alco C-628, 62
Alco C-630, 62
Alco C-636, 62
Alco Century Series, 62
Alco FA-1, 102
Alco FA-2, 102
Alco FPA, 102
Alco M640, 62
Alco PA-1, 102
Alco PA-2, 102
Alco PA-3, 102
Alco RS1, 20
Alco RS2, 20
Alco RS3, 20
Alco RS11, 26
Alco RS27, 26
Alco RS32, 26
Alco RS36, 26
Alco RSC2, 20
Alco RSC3, 20
Alco RSD1, 20
Alco RSD4, 20
Alco RSD5, 20
Alco RSD12, 50
Alco RSD15, 50
Alco RSD17, 50
Alco S-1, 6
Alco S-2, 6

Alco S-3, 6
Alco S-4, 6
Alco S-5, 6
Alco S-6, 6
Alco T-6, 6
ALP44, ABB, 110
AMD-103 Genesis, GE, 96
AMD-110 Genesis, GE, 96
Amfleet passenger cars, 118,
   120
Amtrak/GE P32-8BWH, 76
AS-16, Baldwin, 24
AS-416, Baldwin, 24
AS-616, Baldwin, 24
AT&SF SF30C, 66
auto carriers, 122
B23-7, GE, 46
B30-7, GE, 46
B30-7A, GE, 46
B30-7A1, GE, 46
B32-8, GE, 48
B32-8WH, GE, 76
B36-7, GE, 46
B39-8, GE, 48
B40-8, GE, 48
B40-8, GE, 76
Baldwin AS-16, 24
Baldwin AS-416, 24
Baldwin AS-616, 24
Baldwin DRS-4-4-15, 24
Baldwin DRS-6-4-15, 24
Baldwin DRS-6-6-15, 24
Baldwin DS-4-4-6, 8
Baldwin DS-4-4-10, 8
Baldwin S-8, 8
Baldwin S-12, 8

Baldwin VO 660, 8
Baldwin VO 1000, 8
bay-window caboose, 128
BL2, EMD, 104
Bombardier HR412, 74
Bombardier HR616, 106
boxcars, 126
BQ23-7, GE, 46
Budd Amfleet passenger cars, 118, 120
bulkhead flatcars, 122
C-420, Alco, 26
C-424, Alco, 40
C-425, Alco, 40
C-430, Alco, 40
C-628, Alco, 62
C-630, Alco, 62
C-636, Alco, 62
C30-7, GE, 66
C30-7A, GE, 66
C32-8, GE, 68
C36-7, GE, 66
C39-8, GE, 68
C39-8E, GE, 68
C40-8, GE, 70
C40-8M, GE, 106
C40-8W, GE, 82
C40-9, GE, 70
C41-8W, GE, 82
C44-9W, GE, 82
caboose, 128
Centennial DD40AX, EMD, 86
centerbeam flatcars, 122
Century Series, Alco, 62
CF7, EMD/AT&SF, 38
covered gondolas, 124
covered hoppers, 124
cupola caboose, 128
cylindrical hoppers, 124
DD40AX Centennial, EMD, 86
depressed center flatcars, 122
Draper Taper, 106
DRS-4-4-15, Baldwin, 24
DRS-6-4-15, Baldwin, 24
DRS-6-6-15, Baldwin, 24
DS-4-4-10, Baldwin, 8
DS-4-4-6, Baldwin, 8
E44, GE, 114
E60CH, EMD, 112

E60CP, EMD, 112
E7, EMD, 100
E8, EMD, 100
E9, EMD, 100
Electro-motive Division see EMD,
EMD AEM7, 110
EMD BL2, 104
EMD DD40AX Centennial, 86
EMD E60CH, 112
EMD E60CP, 112
EMD E7, 100
EMD E8, 100
EMD E9, 100
EMD F series, 98
EMD F3, 98
EMD F7, 98
EMD F9, 98
EMD F40C, 88
EMD F40PH, 92
EMD F40PH-2, 92
EMD F40PH-2C, 92
EMD F40PHM-2, 92
EMD F40PHR, 92
EMD F59PH, 94
EMD F59PHI, 94
EMD F69PH-AC, 96
EMD FL9, 100
EMD FP7, 98
EMD FP9, 98
EMD FP45, 90
EMD GF6C, 112
EMD GMD1, 22
EMD GP7, 28
EMD GP9, 28
EMD GP15-1, 30
EMD GP15T, 30
EMD GP18, 28
EMD GP20, 30
EMD GP28, 32
EMD GP30, 32
EMD GP35, 32
EMD GP38, 34
EMD GP38-2, 34
EMD GP38-2W, 74
EMD GP39, 34
EMD GP39-2, 34
EMD GP39X, 34
EMD GP40, 36
EMD GP40-2, 36

EMD GP40-2W, 74
EMD GP40P, 36
EMD GP40X, 36
EMD GP49, 34
EMD GP50, 38
EMD GP59, 38
EMD GP60, 38
EMD GP60M, 76
EMD MP15, 11, 18
EMD MP15(DC), 18
EMD MP15AC, 18
EMD MP15T, 11, 18
EMD NC1, 10
EMD NC2, 10
EMD NW1, 10
EMD NW2, 10, 12
EMD NW3, 10
EMD NW4, 10
EMD NW5, 10, 12
EMD RS1325, 22
EMD SC, 10
EMD SD7, 50
EMD SD9, 50
EMD SD18, 50
EMD SD24, 50
EMD SD28, 52
EMD SD35, 52
EMD SD38, 52
EMD SD38-2, 52
EMD SD39, 54
EMD SD40, 56
EMD SD40-2(W), 78
EMD SD40-2F, 108
EMD SD40A, 56
EMD SD40T-2, 60
EMD SD40X, 58
EMD SD45, 58
EMD SD45-2, 58
EMD SD45T-2, 60
EMD SD50, 72
EMD SD50F, 108
EMD SD60, 72
EMD SD60F, 108
EMD SD60I, 78
EMD SD60M, 78
EMD SD60MAC, 80
EMD SD70, 72
EMD SD70M, 80
EMD SD70MAC, 80
EMD SD75M, 80
EMD SD80MAC, 80

EMD SD90MAC, 80
EMD SDL39, 54
EMD SDP35, 52
EMD SDP40, 56
EMD SDP40F, 88, 90
EMD SDP45, 58
EMD SW, 10
EMD SW1, 10, 12
EMD SW7, 10, 14
EMD SW8, 10, 14
EMD SW9, 10, 14
EMD SW600, 10, 14
EMD SW900, 10, 14
EMD SW1000, 11, 16
EMD SW1001, 11, 16
EMD SW1200, 10, 14
EMD SW1500, 11, 16
EMD SW1504, 11, 16
EMD TR2, 10
EMD TR4, 10
EMD TR5, 12
EMD/AT&SF CF7, 38
EMD/AT&SF SDF45, 90
EMD/AT&SF SDFP45, 90
EMD/AT&SF SDP40-2, 88
EMD/IC GP10, 28
EMD/IC GP11, 28
F series, EMD, 98
F3, EMD, 98
F7, EMD, 98
F9, EMD, 98
F40C, EMD, 88
F40PH, EMD, 92
F40PH-2, EMD, 92
F40PH-2C, EMD, 92
F40PHL-2, Morrison Knudson, 92
F40PHM-2, EMD, 9
F40PHM-2C, Morrison Knudson, 92
F40PHR, EMD, 92
F59PH, EMD, 94
F59PHI, EMD, 94
F69PH AC, EMD, 96
FA-1, Alco, 102
FA-2, Alco, 102
Fairbanks-Morse H-10-44, 18
Fairbanks-Morse H-12-44, 18
FL9, EMD, 100

flatcars, 122
FP7, EMD, 98
FP9, EMD, 98
FP45, EMD, 90
FPA, Alco, 102
GE AC4400CW, 84
GE AC6000CW, 84
GE AMD-103 Genesis, 96
GE AMD-110 Genesis, 96
GE B23-7, 46
GE B30-7, 46
GE B30-7A, 46
GE B30-7A1, 46
GE B32-8, 48
GE B32-8WH, 76
GE B36-7, 46
GE B39-8, 48
GE B40-8, 48
GE B40-8W, 76
GE BQ23-7, 46
GE C30-7, 66
GE C30-7A, 66
GE C32-8, 68
GE C36-7, 66
GE C39-8, 68
GE C39-8E, 68
GE C40-8, 70
GE C40-8M, 106
GE C40-8W, 82
GE C40-9, 70
GE C41-8W, 82
GE C44-9W, 82
GE Dash-7 series, 66
GE Dash-8 series, 68, 70, 76,
    82, 106
GE Dash-9 series, 70, 82
GE E44, 114
GE P32, 76
GE P32-8WH, 76
GE P32AC-DM Genesis, 96
GE P40-BWH Genesis, 96
GE Super 7, 70
GE U-boats, 42, 44, 64, 66
GE U18B, 44
GE U23B, 44
GE U23C, 64
GE U25B, 42
GE U25C, 64
GE U28B, 42
GE U28C, 64
GE U30B, 42

GE U30C, 64
GE U33B, 44
GE U33C, 64
GE U36B, 44
GE U36C, 64
GE/AT&SF SF30C, 66
General Electric see GE
General Motors see EMD
Genesis, AMD-103, AMD-
    110, GE, 96
GF6C, EMD, 112
GMD1, EMD, 22
gondolas, 124
GP7, EMD, 28
GP9, EMD, 28
GP10, EMD/IC, 28
GP11, EMD/IC, 28
GP15-1, EMD, 30
GP15T, EMD, 30
GP18, EMD, 28
GP18, EMD, 28
GP20, EMD, 30
GP28, EMD, 32
GP30, EMD, 32
GP35, EMD, 23
GP38, EMD, 34
GP38-2, EMD, 34
GP38-2W, EMD, 74
GP39, EMD, 34
GP39-2, EMD, 34
GP39X, EMD, 34
GP40, EMD, 36
GP40-2, EMD, 36
GP40-2W, EMD, 74
GP40FH-2, Morrison Knud-
    son, 92
GP40P, EMD, 36
GP40X, EMD, 36
GP49, EMD, 34
GP50, EMD, 38
GP59, EMD, 38
GP60, EMD, 38
GP60M, EMD, 76
H-10-44, Fairbanks-Morse,
    18
H-12-44, Fairbanks-Morse,
    18
Heritage Fleet passenger cars,
    118
hi-level Superliner passenger
    cars, 118, 120

hopper cars, 124
Horizon passenger car, 118, 120
HR412, Bombardier, 74
HR616, Bombardier, 106
intermodal service, 122
livestock cars, 126
LRC, 116
M420(W), MLW, 74
M420R, MLW, 74
M630, MLW, 62
M636, MLW, 62
M640, Alco, 62
MK Viewliner passenger cars, 118, 120
MK1200G, Morrison Knudson, 24
MK5000C, Morrison Knudson, 84
MLW M420(W), 74
MLW M420R, 74
MLW M630, 62
MLW M636, 62
MLW S-11, 8
MLW S-12, 8
MLW S-13, 8
Montreal Locomotive Works *see* MLW
Morrison Knudson F40PHL-2, 92
Morrison Knudson F40PHM-2C, 92
Morrison Knudson GP40FH-2, 92
Morrison Knudson MK1200G, 24
Morrison Knudson MK5000C, 84
MP15(DC), EMD, 18
MP15, EMD, 11, 18
MP15AC, EMD, 18
MP15T, EMD, 11, 18
NC1, EMD, 10
NC2, EMD, 10
NW1, EMD, 10
NW2, EMD, 10, 12
NW3, EMD, 10
NW4, EMD, 10
NW5, EMD, 10, 12
P32, GE, 76
P32-8BWH, Amtrak/GE, 76

P32-8WH, GE, 76
P32AC-DM Genesis, GE, 96
P40-BWH Genesis, GE, 96
PA-1, Alco, 102
PA-2, Alco, 102
PA-3, Alco, 102
piggybacking, 122
refrigerated boxcars, 126
Rohr Turboliner, 116
rotary-dump gondolas, 124
RS1, Alco, 20
RS2, Alco, 20
RS3, Alco, 20
RS11, Alco, 26
RS27, Alco, 26
RS32, Alco, 26
RS36, Alco, 26
RS1325, EMD, 22
RSC2, Alco, 20
RSC3, Alco, 20
RSD1, Alco, 20
RSD4, Alco, 20
RSD5, Alco, 20
RSD12,Alco, 50
RSD15, Alco, 50
RSD17, Alco, 50
S-1, Alco, 6
S-2, Alco, 6
S-3, Alco , 6
S-4, Alco, 6
S-5, Alco, 6
S-6, Alco, 6
S-8, Baldwin, 8
S-11, MLW, 8
S-12, Baldwin, 8
S-12, MLW, 8
S-13, MLW, 8
SC, EMD, 10
SD7, EMD, 50
SD9, EMD, 50
SD18, EMD, 50
SD24, EMD, 50
SD28, EMD, 52
SD35, EMD, 52
SD38, EMD, 52
SD38-2, EMD, 52
SD39, EMD, 54
SD40, EMD, 56
SD40-2(W). EMD, 78
SD40-2F, EMD, 108
SD40A, EMD, 56

SD40T-2, EMD, 60
SD40X, EMD, 58
SD45, EMD, 58
SD45-2, EMD, 58
SD45T-2, EMD, 60
SD50, EMD, 72
SD50F, EMD, 108
SD60, EMD, 72
SD60F, EMD, 108
SD60I, EMD, 78
SD60M, EMD, 78
SD60MAC, EMD, 80
SD70, EMD, 72
SD70M, EMD, 80
SD70MAC, EMD, 80
SD75M, EMD, 80
SD80MAC, EMD, 80
SD90MAC, EMD, 80
SDF45, EMD/ATSF, 90
SDFP45, EMD/AT&SF, 90
SDL39, EMD, 54
SDP35, EMD, 52
SDP40, EMD, 56
SDP40-2, EMD/AT&SF, 88
SDP40F, EMD, 88, 90
SDP45, EMD, 58
SF30C, GE/AT&SF, 66
spine car, 122
Super 7, GE, 70
Superliner passenger cars,
    118, 120
SW, EMD, 10
SW1, EMD, 10, 12
SW7, EMD, 10, 14
SW8, EMD, 10, 14
SW9, EMD, 10, 14
SW600, EMD, 10, 14
SW900, EMD, 10, 14
SW1000, EMD, 11, 16
SW1001, EMD, 11, 16
SW1200, EMD, 10, 14
SW1500, EMD, 11, 16
SW1504, EMD, 11, 16
T-6, Alco, 6
tank cars, 126
TR2, EMD, 10
TR4, EMD, 10, 14
TR5, EMD, 12
Turboliner, Rohr, 116
U-boats, 42, 44, 64, 66
U18B, GE, 44

U23B, GE, 44
U23C, GE, 64
U25B, GE, 42
U25C, GE, 64
U28B, GE, 42
U28C, GE, 64
U30B, GE, 42
U30C, GE, 64
U33B, GE, 44
U33C, GE, 64
U36B, GE, 44
U36C, GE, 64
Viewliner passenger cars,
    118, 120
VO 660, Baldwin, 8
VO 1000, Baldwin, 8
well car, 122
wide cupola caboose, 128
wood chip gondolas, 124